Bystanders to
the Vietnam War

Bystanders to the Vietnam War

*The Role of the
United States Senate,
1950–1965*

Ronald Allen Goldberg

McFarland & Company, Inc., Publishers
Jefferson, North Carolina

LIBRARY OF CONGRESS CATALOGUING-IN-PUBLICATION DATA

Names: Goldberg, Ronald Allen, author.
Title: Bystanders to the Vietnam War : the role of the United States Senate, 1950–1965 / Ronald Allen Goldberg.
Description: Jefferson, North Carolina : McFarland & Company, Inc., Publishers, 2018 | Includes bibliographical references and index.
Identifiers: LCCN 2018035833 | ISBN 9781476668918 (softcover : acid free paper) ∞
Subjects: LCSH: Vietnam War, 1961–1975—United States. | United States. Congress. Senate—History—20th century.
Classification: LCC DS558 .G63 2018 | DDC 959.704/310973—dc23
LC record available at https://lccn.loc.gov/2018035833

BRITISH LIBRARY CATALOGUING DATA ARE AVAILABLE

ISBN (print) 978-1-4766-6891-8
ISBN (ebook) 978-1-4766-3378-7

© 2018 Ronald Allen Goldberg. All rights reserved

No part of this book may be reproduced or transmitted in any form or by any means, electronic or mechanical, including photocopying or recording, or by any information storage and retrieval system, without permission in writing from the publisher.

Front cover image of U.S. Capitol building in Washington, D.C. (© 2018 Ed-Ni-Photo/iStock); photograph of troops moving across a rice field in search of Viet Cong (Department of Defense / Department of the Army / Office of the Deputy Chief of Staff for Operations / National Archives)

Printed in the United States of America

McFarland & Company, Inc., Publishers
  Box 611, Jefferson, North Carolina 28640
    www.mcfarlandpub.com

Table of Contents

Preface 1

I. Historical Introduction 3

II. The Years of Growing Involvement 14

III. The Decision Not to Intervene 31

IV. The Creation of the Southeast Asia Treaty Organization 45

V. The Geneva Conference 58

VI. The Quiet Years 71

VII. The Kennedy Years 84

VIII. The Tonkin Gulf Affair 100

IX. The Decision to Escalate 117

X. Conclusions 131

Chapter Notes 135

Bibliography 141

Index 145

Preface

Benjamin Franklin once declared, "Victory has 100 fathers; defeat is an orphan," and President John F. Kennedy borrowed the phrase at a news conference, April 21, 1961.

These words apply to the Vietnam War, probably the most controversial conflict in American history. Did the U.S. Senate share responsibility for the war with the three U.S. presidents, Eisenhower, Kennedy, and Johnson, who were in office as the American role in Vietnam steadily grew? Did each of these three presidents play an important role in committing the nation to defending Vietnam, or was this important decision mainly the action of President Johnson?

The Vietnam War clearly demonstrates the interaction of the Senate and the presidency in shaping foreign policy. This quest for determining U.S. foreign policy goes back to the earliest days of the republic. This has resulted in alternating periods of foreign policy supremacy between these two branches of government. On the crucial question of declaring war, the president has usually maintained the upper hand. This tendency was clearly demonstrated as the United States became more involved in Vietnam, ultimately culminating in the decision to launch a major war in 1965.

The Vietnam quagmire, which emerged soon after the end of World War II in 1945, was only the second time America became heavily involved in a Third World guerrilla insurgency. (The United States fought an insurrection in the Philippines from 1899 to 1902, shortly after annexing the islands following the Spanish-American War.) With the possible exception of Senator Mike Mansfield of Montana, no "expert" ever emerged on the situation in Vietnam. For most of the period after 1945, few in the Senate ever became extensively engaged in the problem, understandable in view of the numerous other crises which emerged at this time. The problems with Communist Eastern Europe, Western attempts

Preface

to retain influence in Greece and Turkey, and especially in Western Europe, overshadowed the developing crisis in Vietnam. Also, the major crises in China and Korea shortly after the end of World War II seemed more crucial than events in Vietnam. Later, Cuba became an important concern.

Not only the Senate, but also the U.S. presidents during the post–World War II period, were generally uninformed about the nature of the Vietnam problem. None saw it reaching such a level of involvement which it ultimately did in the 1960s. Generally in dealing with the problem, the president had essentially a "free hand" as the U.S. Senate was uninformed about Vietnam or was reluctant to challenge the president during a difficult time.

If the U.S. involvement in the Vietnam War was basically a presidential decision, which president was mainly responsible? President Johnson claimed he was merely continuing the policies of former presidents Eisenhower and Kennedy. Reluctant to challenge a sitting president, Eisenhower refused to comment on the matter except in 1966 when he declared he had only promised economic aid to South Vietnam, and not U.S. military protection. The evidence indicates that President Kennedy, at the time of his death in 1963, had never decided whether or not to launch a war in Vietnam. It seems therefore that primary responsibility for the war in Vietnam should be placed with President Johnson, rather than his immediate predecessors or the U.S. Senate.

The Senate's role was clearly a secondary one as the crisis in Vietnam grew larger. This study shows the feelings of many of the leading senators, in their own words, concerning Vietnam during the 1950s and '60s. As during most of American history, on the crucial decision of waging war, the Senate was ultimately overshadowed by the president. This question of which branch of government has the major responsibility for waging war has continued into the current period, as the nation weighs an ever-increasing role in the Middle East and Afghanistan.

I

Historical Introduction

Congressional versus executive initiative in foreign affairs is a controversy which predates even the creation of the United States government. All of American history has been marked by the shifting ebb and flow of power in this area between these two branches of government. Generally, Congress was in control, but during times of crisis the initiative tended to shift to the executive. In recent times, with crisis following close upon crisis, the executive has seemingly emerged the victor over the Senate in this contest for primacy.

Commenting on this problem in the 1830s, Alexis de Tocqueville, the French traveler and writer, noted in his *Democracy in America*: "It is especially in the conduct of their foreign relations [that] democracies appear to me decidedly inferior to other governments.... Foreign politics demand scarcely any of those qualities which are peculiar to a democracy; they require, on the contrary, the perfect use of almost all those in which it is deficient."[1] He believed the conduct of foreign affairs required a strong, firm grip at the helm rather than the diffused power of a democracy.

Glancing at the Constitution, it is easy to see why this distinguished author could feel that a clear mandate to conduct foreign affairs for the executive was lacking. The colonial period had been dominated by the struggle for supremacy between the royal governors and the colonial legislatures. As a consequence, noted English philosopher John Locke's theory of legislative supremacy came to be widely accepted by the Revolutionary patriots.[2] "When [the colonial] background is considered," wrote historian Denna Fleming, "the executive [under the Articles] was perhaps fortunate ... to get the power to shake hands with foreign ambassadors and to write letters abroad."[3] Functioning under the Articles of Confederation, the Continental Congress retained within itself major powers of conducting foreign affairs, such as the determination of war and peace, making treaties, and appointing foreign ministers. Clearly, under the Articles, the legislative branch had attained primacy in foreign affairs.

At the Constitutional Convention in 1787, a strong effort by Alexander Hamilton and James Madison on behalf of a stronger executive role was somewhat responsible for a more equitable distribution of power over foreign affairs between the two branches of government.[4] Ostensibly, the most important foreign relations were left largely legislative. The power to declare war, to define piracies and offenses against the law of nations and to regulate foreign commerce were left with Congress. The power to make treaties and to appoint ambassadors, public ministers and consuls was made to require the consent of the Senate. The executive's powers generally were outlined in three areas: he was authorized to act as commander-in-chief of the armed forces and of the militia when called into active service; to make treaties with Senate concurrence; and to appoint ministers to foreign countries and to receive ambassadors from other countries.

This overall arrangement was flexible enough to permit the executive, at certain periods, to seize the initiative in foreign affairs. The constitutional fathers had deliberately made vague the delineation between executive and legislative powers in this area, thus creating what historian Edward Corwin has called "an invitation to struggle."[5] They were torn between their unhappy past experience with royal executive power and the obvious need for a firm hand to conduct foreign affairs of the new nation.

The administration of George Washington provided the trial for this new constitutional arrangement. The first major test occurred in 1789 concerning the treaty with the southern Indians. Washington interpreted the constitutional provision of advice and consent literally to require his presence at the Senate chambers; yet, when the president arrived, the Senate decided it was not ready to deal with the matter and voted to recommit the papers communicated by the president to a committee of five. Senator Maclay of Pennsylvania noted in his journal: "The president of the United States started up in a violent threat. 'This defeats every purpose of my coming here' were the first words that he said. He then went on to say that he had brought his secretary of war with him to give every necessary information; that the secretary knew all about the business, and yet he was delayed and could not go on with the matter."[6] Washington went back to the Senate several days later. Leaving in a rage, he swore never to return.

I. Historical Introduction

Neither he nor any other president ever appeared before the Senate to testify on pending treaties.

Another test occurred when the president issued his Neutrality Proclamation of 1793 during the war between England and France which had just broken out. The Republicans, who were the opposition political party at the time, claimed that this was a clear case of executive usurpation. Treasury Secretary Alexander Hamilton, replying under the pseudonym of Pacificus, argued that the inherent power of the executive amply qualified him to take the initiative in foreign affairs. "If, on the one hand, the legislature had a right to declare war," he wrote, "it is, on the other hand, the duty of the executive to preserve peace till the declaration is made."[7]

At the urging of Thomas Jefferson, James Madison issued the Republican rebuttal. In his Helvidius letters, Madison contended that the Congress had the basic authority to determine foreign policy; the president could serve only as the channel by which congressional determinations were transmitted to foreign states. Ostensibly, the executive lost this round when the passage of the Neutrality Act of 1794 apparently assured Congress of authority over neutrality matters. (The Neutrality Act of 1794 made it illegal for an American to wage war against any country at peace with the United States. It also forbade foreign war vessels to outfit in American waters, and set a three-mile territorial limit at sea.)

In that same year, the controversy over the Jay Treaty demonstrated the power of Congress to amend treaties. The treaty provided for the adjustment of important difficulties with Great Britain and by the 12th article greatly restricted the export trade of the United States. On June 24, 1795, the Senate advised and consented to a ratification of the treaty "on condition" that an article be added to the treaty suspending the operation of that part of the 12th article which related to the trade between the United States and the British West Indies. After conferring with his cabinet, Washington decided to accept this amended form of the treaty. The suspension of the operation of this questionable 12th article in the Jay treaty was agreed to by the British government, albeit not gladly, and the ratifications of the treaty were exchanged at London, October 18, 1795. By the end of his second term in office, Washington had clearly defended the executive's privileges in foreign affairs, although he had not attained the degree of primacy in this area which later presidents would possess.

Under the subsequent administrations of presidents Adams and Jefferson, the trend toward greater executive hegemony in foreign policy developed. Adams, under pressure from his own party to declare war on the French in 1798, stood his ground and ultimately avoided war. Jefferson, overcoming previous reservations of a too-powerful role by the president, now termed the conduct of foreign affairs "executive altogether," and demonstrated his initiative by making war on the Barbary pirates without congressional authorization. In his first annual message, he reported his actions in Tripoli. "The style of the demand [for tribute] admitted but one answer. I sent a small squadron of frigates into the Mediterranean."[8]

In succeeding years, this contest for the foreign policy initiative swayed back and forth. The vacillating President Madison was forced by the War Hawks, a militant faction in Congress, to declare war on Britain in 1812. But his successor, James Monroe, demonstrated a greater concept of the executive's foreign policy role. Monroe and Congress clashed over the recognition of the Latin American republics. When Congress tried to move into Hemisphere policy through Clay's effort in 1818 to hurry Monroe into recognizing the revolutionary government of Argentina, or later when the opponents of the Panama Congress tried to tack on conditions to the appropriations for the mission, the result was a vigorous and uncompromising defense of the presidential authority. (Revolutionary leader Simon Bolivar had called the meeting to create an organization of the newly independent countries in the Western Hemisphere.)

On the other hand, the powers of the Senate had been enhanced in 1817 when the British questioned the validity of the Rush-Bagot agreement providing for naval limitations on the Great Lakes between the two nations. England feared that it might not bind later administrations unless it was approved by the Senate. Consequently, it was submitted to the Senate which approved it unanimously on April 16, 1818.

The most dramatic example of presidential initiative during Monroe's presidency was his issuance of the Monroe Doctrine. Monroe did consult with his cabinet and with such elder statesman as Jefferson and Madison before promulgating the doctrine, but handed down the policy to Congress as an accomplished fact. The doctrine forbade further European colonization in the Western Hemisphere as well as the transferring of existing colonies from one European country to another. One congressman called the doctrine "an unauthorized, unmeaning, and empty menace"; another declared that is assumed an "unwarrantable power." Of course, the doctrine did not impress foreign nations either in 1823.

When compared to the initiatives demonstrated by later presidents,

I. Historical Introduction

Monroe's actions seem mild. The years between Monroe and Tyler were described by historian Thomas Bailey as the "awkward period in American diplomacy." But by the 1840s, the Texas question had become the source of a major conflict between the presidency and the Senate. When President John Tyler in 1844 attempted to have the Senate ratify a treaty annexing Texas, that body thwarted his wishes. Soon after Congress, by joint resolution, did annex Texas, and simultaneously greatly disturbed the already tense diplomatic setting with Mexico.

At this juncture began the administration of President James Polk whose tenure in office demonstrated executive initiative in foreign affairs at its highest degree up to that time. Polk believed in the technique of a fait accompli foreign policy. The United States and Mexico strongly disagreed on the boundary between Texas and its southern neighbor. Polk fomented a crisis with Mexico when he occupied the disputed area, and subsequently settled the Texas question on terms extremely favorable to the United States. Polk's Texas initiative, which led to a war with Mexico, evoked vigorous outcry in Congress. A young congressman from Illinois, Abraham Lincoln, issued a resolution demanding to know at exactly what "spot" the Mexican troops had crossed into American territory and provoked the American counterattack.[9]

In the Senate, the Texas question led to a vigorous debate. In his message to Congress, Polk had stated: "Mexico has passed the boundary of the United States, has invaded its territory and shed American blood upon the American soil. She has proclaimed that hostilities have commenced and that the two nations are now at war. As war exists, [it is] by the act of Mexico herself."[10] Senator John C. Calhoun then engaged in a colloquy with fellow senator Lewis Cass on the war-making power of Congress. Calhoun stated that under the Constitution, war could only be declared by Congress. Cass dissented with a pragmatic argument. "It is certain that Congress alone has the right to declare war.... But another country can commence a war against us without the cooperation of Congress.... War may be commenced with or without a previous declaration.... All these facts prove conclusively that it is a state of hostilities that produces war, and not the formal declaration."[11]

Once the Texas question was resolved, the issue of presidential initiative tended to become quiescent for the next decade and a half until Abraham Lincoln's presidency. Congress had seemingly attained the initiative on domestic events as well as in foreign policy. When President Pierce attempted to buy Cuba in 1855, he was blocked by the Congress.

Bystanders to the Vietnam War

Weak presidents until 1860 were the rule as the nation, grappling with the terribly complex problem of slavery, avoided a strong executive who might plunge the country into civil war.

This situation continued until the election of Lincoln whose presidency was a portent of future constitutional developments. Unquestionably, the high water mark in the exercise of executive power in the United States during its first century was in the administration of Lincoln. His seemingly unlimited view of executive powers he defended by insisting, "My oath to preserve the Constitution imposed on me the duty of preserving by every indispensable means that government, that nation of which the Constitution was the organic law. Was it possible to lose the nation and yet preserve the Constitution?... I felt that measures, otherwise unconstitutional might become lawful by becoming indispensable to the preservation of the Constitution through the preservation of the nation."[12] This eloquent explanation remains one of the finest defenses of the expansion of executive powers during a national emergency. Lincoln's broad view of his domestic powers carried over into foreign affairs. He refused to let Congress force his hand regarding the French occupation of Mexico in 1862. That problem, he correctly foresaw, would have to wait until the end of the Civil War.

Between the presidency of Lincoln and the end of the century, the Senate maintained the upper hand in foreign policy as well as in domestic events. When President Ulysses Grant attempted to purchase Santa Domingo (Haiti), he was blocked by Senator Charles Sumner who ruled the foreign affairs of the nation with the airs of a "Roman triumvir." Powerful senators such as George Hoar correctly affirmed that the Senate had control of the reins of government. He commented, "The most eminent senators would have received as a personal affront a private message from the White House expressing a desire that they adopt any course in the discharge of their legislative duties that they did not approve. If they visited the White House, it was to give, not to receive, advice. Each of these stars kept his own orbit in his sphere, within which he tolerated no intrusion from the president or from anybody else."[13]

One of the most literate evaluators of the American political scene at that time, the young Woodrow Wilson, noticed the diminished role of the presidency. In 1879, he wrote in the *North American Review*: "The president can seldom make himself recognized as a leader. He is merely the executor of the sovereign legislative will; his cabinet officers are little

I. Historical Introduction

more than the chief clerks or superintendents in the executive departments, who advise the president as to matters in most of which he has no power of action independently of the concurrence of the Senate."[14]

Beginning with the administration of President Grover Cleveland, the political balance began noticeably to shift again. Cleveland, standing on his prerogatives, blocked the Senate's initiatives toward Hawaii and Cuba. The Senate was interested in annexing Hawaii, and later in intervening in the Cuban revolt against Spanish rule, steps that Cleveland opposed.

The presidency of his successor, William McKinley, was marked by several notable conflicts between the Congress and the executive. In 1897, the Olney-Pauncefote Treaty, which provided for the arbitration of disputes between the United States and Great Britain failed of ratification in the Senate and resulted in much hard feeling with England. Regarding the turbulent days prior to the Spanish-American war, there is still an unsettled question concerning the extent to which McKinley followed or directed congressional initiative with a declaration of war with Spain. The Hay-Pauncefote Treaty in 1900, relating to the proposed Panama Canal, was amended by the Senate, much to the dismay of Great Britain. This contest for the foreign policy initiative, which was in doubt in the last decade of the nineteenth century, was clearly won by several strong presidents in the following century.

Under the reign of Theodore Roosevelt, the modern vigorous presidency clearly developed. The emergence of a national economy was creating social and economic problems, requiring national policies. In addition, the emergence of the United States as a world power was creating foreign problems, requiring national leadership to defend the national interest. These developments imposed new demands on the national government, especially on the president's conduct of foreign affairs.

Writing in 1900, Woodrow Wilson reflected upon these changes. "Much of the most important change to be noticed is the result of the war with Spain upon the lodgment and exercise of power within our federal system; the greatly increased power and opportunity for constructive statesmanship given the president by the plunge into international politics.... When foreign affairs play a prominent part in the politics of the nation, its executive must of necessity be its guide; must utter every initial judgment, take every first step of action, supply the information upon which it is to act, suggest and in large measure, control its conduct."[15]

Bystanders to the Vietnam War

Theodore Roosevelt fitted this mode of president. His theory of the "stewardship" presidency envisioned the chief executive as a vigorous leader. Essentially this thesis stated his view that "every executive officer was the steward of the people, bound actively and affirmatively to do all he could for the people, and not to content himself with the negative merit of keeping his talents undamaged in a napkin."[16] Expressing words applicable to Lincoln's philosophy, Roosevelt added: "The most important factor in getting the right spirit in my administration was my insistence upon the theory that the executive power was limited only by specific restrictions and prohibitions appearing in the Constitution or imposed by Congress under its constitutional powers. I did not usurp power but I did greatly broaden the use of executive power."[17] Roosevelt acted upon this theory in his foreign policy by involving himself in international disputes, fomenting a crisis with Columbia, and sending the fleet around the world while daring the Congress not to appropriate funds for its return. His Roosevelt Corollary to the Monroe Doctrine, making the United States an international policeman in the Western Hemisphere, with the right to intervene when necessary, was a major expansion of the president's conduct in foreign affairs.

The most striking personifiers of the bold presidential initiative between Roosevelt and the onset of World War II were presidents Woodrow Wilson and Franklin Roosevelt. Wilson believed in a loose interpretation of the president's powers so that "the office would be as big as the man who filled it." Refusing to be deterred by a band of "willful senators," he continued the policies which led the United States into World War I. Wilson made this comment when a small group of senators filibustered his bill to arm merchant ships. Through existing statutes, he was able to achieve this policy anyway. To his dismay, he learned that the executive's initiative had certain limits as shown by the Senate's rejection of the Treaty of Versailles, ending World War I.

Franklin Roosevelt also had his troubles with the Senate over foreign relations. His attempt to have the United States Senate adhere to the World Court was blocked. Furthermore, on the very eve of World War II, the Senate Foreign Relations Committee thwarted his wishes to repeal the Neutrality Acts.

By 1940, the situation had changed drastically as the nation approached its most severe military crisis since the Civil War. Roosevelt responded with vigorous executive leadership. A paramount example was his use of

I. Historical Introduction

executive agreements, such as the Destroyers Deal with Great Britain, which led many to claim that Roosevelt was usurping congressional powers. In two decisions, the Supreme Court upheld the use of executive agreements. In the 1936 Curtiss-Wright decision, the Court ruled there was virtually a limitless range for executive agreements. In the 1937 Belmont decision, the Court decided that executive agreements must be regarded as the law of the land. Even some of Congress' specifically authorized bills such as the Lend Lease Act also tended greatly to increase the executive's power. As evident by all the other instances of national danger, the nation acquiesced as the president seemed best able to cope with the emergency.

The post–1940 increase in the executive's foreign policy powers reflects the very structure of the national government. Although the constitutional boundary line between the responsibilities of the Senate and the president is vague, the development of the "age of crisis" inevitably led to a shift toward presidential initiative. This development reflects the president's possessing both an intellectual and instrumental initiative over the Senate. His intellectual initiative rests on such organizations as the Central Intelligence Agency (CIA), the Federal Bureau of Investigation (FBI), the Army and Navy intelligence groups, the diplomatic corps, and the better staffing of the presidency which give him the information needed to act quickly. Furthermore, the president's control of the flow of information enables him to set up the ground rules for debate and action on terms most favorable to his policies. This ability of the president to act "quickly" and with "dispatch" was even cited by John Jay in the 64th *Federalist* back in 1788.

The president's instrumental initiative reflects his greater freedom of movement in international affairs. For example, he can negotiate executive agreements, thus presenting the Senate with a fait accompli which could only be rejected at the price of diminishing the prestige of the presidency and the nation. Also, the diversity of the Senate creates a division of power which makes it more difficult, if not impossible, for that body to seize the initiative and act quickly in critical times. In addition, the Senate's collective will to act is often thwarted by individual senators who wish to please the president and will defer to his policies. Even when unified, the Senate has been virtually unable to substitute its own policy for that of the executive. To do this, senators would have to win public opinion; yet modern presidents have tended to make skillful use of the mass media to shape public opinion.

Bystanders to the Vietnam War

The most striking example of the executive's instrumental initiative has been his use of the war-making power. James Madison, reflecting upon the Constitutional Convention, wrote: "The Constitution supposes what the history of all governments demonstrates, that the executive is the branch of power most interested in war and most prone to it. It has accordingly, with studied care, vested the question of war in the legislature."[18] When the Constitution was being written, there was a realization that the British government in colonial times had abused the war-making power. According to historian Ruhl Batlett: "The framers of the Constitution knew the power of the British Crown to declare war and drag the British people into foreign adventures that exacted their sacrifices and stole their liberties. and they did not propose to give the same power to an American president."[19]

Thomas Jefferson also believed that the Congress, rather than the executive, was a more responsible body on the question of war and peace. He wrote: "The Constitution provided an effectual check to the 'dogs of war' by transferring the power of letting him loose from the executive to the legislative body, from those who are to spend to those who are to pay."[20] Yet there have been more than 125 instances where the president has used United States troops without congressional authorization. Although the Constitution vests in Congress the power to declare war, the United States has declared war in only five of its eleven major conflicts with other nations. In each of the five instances Congress declared war only in response to the president's acts or recommendations.

During the twentieth century, the war-making power has shifted even more toward the executive. Without a congressional declaration of war, Truman launched the Korean War, Johnson, the war in Vietnam, and George W. Bush, the wars in Iraq and Afghanistan. Congress has not formally declared war since the Pearl Harbor attack in December 1941.

In the post–World War II era, with the United States continually on the verge of war, the executive's primacy in international affairs has continued to increase. Various writings of Senator J. William Fulbright, perhaps the Senate's authority on foreign affairs, recognized this trend and defended it. Fulbright, in the pre–Vietnam era, firmly declared that foreign policy should be initiated by the president. He stated that the Senate's responsibility was to explain the burdens of international policies to the public and make them more tolerable, but that the primary responsibility should lie with the president. Fulbright stated: "It seems to me that in for-

I. Historical Introduction

eign affairs, the Senate cannot initiate or force large events or substitute its judgment of them for that of the president without seriously jeopardizing the ability of the nation to act consistently, and also without confusing the image and purpose of the country in the eyes of others."[21] Fulbright believed that the Constitution made the president "the leading actor [in foreign affairs], not a spectator and mere witness. It was never intended by the Founding Fathers that the president of the United States should be a ventriloquist dummy sitting on the lap of Congress."[22] Even though the Senate should not indulge in the "frivolous delusion" of co-equality with the president in foreign affairs, Fulbright prophetically cautioned against the danger of fait accompli government which bypassed the Congress and the public. In the immediate post–World War II era and later in the 1960s, this prophecy sadly came to fruition.

II

The Years of Growing Involvement

The post–World War II era in the United States witnessed considerable rancor between the Senate and the executive over the foreign policy initiative. Presidents Roosevelt and Truman had both practiced vigorous leadership in their foreign policies, often without consulting the Congress. By the early 1950s, the deepening Cold War led the Senate to rebel against this executive "tyranny." This conflict became more acute as the United States commitments to Indochina grew. By the end of 1953, there was the possibility that United States combat troops would be engaged. Despite this "revolt" by the Senate, the executive maintained his initiative in foreign policy, although President Eisenhower was more considerate of the Senate's prerogatives than had been his immediate predecessors.

Indochina was originally a French concern, long before the United States ever became involved. In the late 1700s, French missionaries went to this area, ultimately leading to many conversions of the native Buddhist population to Roman Catholicism. The French influence steadily increased, and in the late 1800s, France formally organized the area as a French colony. During World II, the area came under Japanese control. After the war, the Japanese were expelled, and the French asked the United States to help them return to their former colony. A strong independence movement under the Communist Ho Chi Minh had arisen, and the seeds for a future conflict had been sown. Would the French agree to sever their ties with their former colony, or risk war to restore the pre–World War II status quo?

United States policy in Indochina was limited until 1950 and almost totally ignored by the Senate. In 1941, Roosevelt had regarded the Japanese seizure of Indochina as a threatening act; this led to his decision to freeze

II. The Years of Growing Involvement

Japanese assets in the United States as well as instituting a trade embargo, and was directly related to the sequence of events climaxing in the attack on Pearl Harbor.

Roosevelt's original plans for Indochina after the end of World War II were totally different from those later followed by his successors. He was the only president involved with Indochina before the Cold War; consequently, he was able to judge the problem in a more detached, rational manner than his successors. The guiding theme behind his policy was his strong opposition to colonialism. Roosevelt personally disliked French leader Charles DeGaulle, and he also believed France to be a poor colonizer. He claimed that France had "milked" the area and exploited the people of Vietnam.

Roosevelt's policy was enunciated in a 1945 article written by Undersecretary of State Sumner Welles, proposing that the various colonial powers be made more responsible and consider converting their colonies into international trusteeships.[1] He added that all presently dependent peoples recognized by an international organization as being fitted for self-government should be immediately entrusted with that right. At the Yalta Conference in 1945, Roosevelt suggested a trusteeship for Indochina, but this plan ended with his death.

Toward the end of his presidency, Roosevelt had begun to change his position. His ideas on colonialism were criticized by British prime minister Winston Churchill who feared the loss of British colonies after World War II. Furthermore, growing suspicions concerning the Soviet Union's intentions in Europe after the war, led his advisers to urge a more pro–French attitude. French leader Charles DeGaulle was strongly opposed to Roosevelt's trusteeship plan, believing that France must return to Indochina in order to remain a great power. The United States realized that France's support would be needed as part of the Western European alliance after the war, and wished not to offend an important ally. At the time of his death, Roosevelt was backing away from his position on a trusteeship status for Indochina.

Roosevelt, probably as part of his world policeman theory, had earlier suggested that Indochina should come under China's rule. (He considered the idea that in a post–World War II era, the United States, England, the Soviet Union, and China would act as policemen to preserve world order.) However, Chinese leader Chiang Kai-shek rejected this idea. At a press conference on February 23, 1945, Roosevelt stated: "The first thing I asked

Bystanders to the Vietnam War

Chiang was: 'Do you want Indochina?' Chiang said: 'It's no help to us. We don't want it. They are not Chinese. They would not assimilate into the Chinese people.'"[2] This is an ironic aspect of history in light of the Johnson administration's later professed claims that the war in Vietnam was, to a large extent, aimed at blocking Chinese expansion into this area.

When Roosevelt died suddenly, the decision about Indochina was left to new president Harry Truman. Truman decided to help the French return to Vietnam, partly because France was an important ally in Europe. Furthermore, the French economy was in dire straits after the war, and there were fears over a growing Communist movement in the country. A debate over French colonialism might destabilize that nation politically. For these reasons, the United States decided to let France handle the Indochina problem in its own way, and would assist in France's reestablishing its former colony.

Between the death of President Roosevelt in 1945 and the outbreak of the Korean War in 1950, United States interest in Indochina was limited; this reflected the turbulent events both in Europe and in China at this time. In China, the bloody civil war was drawing to a climax. With the fall of the pro–American government and the fate of nearly 500 million people about to be determined, consideration of the Vietnam problem drew little interest in Congress.

One who did speak out on the Indochina issue was former ambassador to Russia, William Bullitt, who sounded the alarm against Vietnamese leader Ho Chi Minh in the December 1947 issue of *Life* magazine.[3] In the Senate, only Senator Ralph Flanders discussed this question with much foresight. He stated in 1950 that "we must persuade ourselves and the French government jointly that purely military operations will never succeed. We must persuade them and ourselves that only popular support will succeed."[4] Ambassador Bullitt's fears prevailed, and Senator Flanders' admonition went unheeded as the fall of China and the deepening Cold War cast a shadow of suspicion over the ambitions of the Communist Ho Chi Minh.

The dominant political figure in Vietnam for many years, Ho had gone to France in 1912 as a very young man and when the Paris Peace Conference in 1919 refused to grant independence for Vietnam, he joined the French Communist Party. Later in 1930, he organized the Indochinese Communist Party. In 1940, after the initial Japanese incursions into Vietnam, Ho returned to his homeland for the first time in nearly thirty years.

II. The Years of Growing Involvement

He was able to eventually organize a sizable army which fought against Japan with U.S. assistance, late in the war. After World War II, he unsuccessfully tried to get France to agree to an independent Vietnam.

In 1946, after a French ship shelled the city of Haiphong, the first Indochina war broke out. Asked by an American news correspondent how he expected to defeat France, a modern power, Ho used his famous analogy of the elephant and the tiger. (When they meet in the open, the elephant will crush the tiger. When they meet in the jungle, the tiger sneaks up on the elephant, rips flesh from its back, and the elephant will bleed to death.)[5] Ho was predicting a guerrilla war in which the more powerful force (France) will eventually bleed to death. Ho was probably encouraged to challenge the French after the Japanese in World War II had greatly weakened the myth of Western invincibility.

The initial American policy in the war was a pro–French "neutrality." The United States supplied financial and military aid to France, ostensibly earmarked for European defense but partly used instead in Indochina. Until 1950, the French were at least not losing the war, when they suffered what a noted historian called France's "greatest colonial defeat since Montcalm died at Quebec (1759)" during the French and Indian War with Great Britain.[6] In the battle of Cao Bay, the French lost over 6,000 men and huge amounts of military supplies. By the end of 1950, the Communists controlled two-thirds of the Vietnamese countryside. They possessed hundreds of thousands of fighters, causing France to suffer about 1,000 casualties each month. This helped initiate the beginning of a long period of expanded military aid to the United States' beleaguered Western ally. The crisis in Vietnam became a major conflict in the Cold War when the newly victorious Chinese Communists began aiding Ho Chi Minh in 1950. Would the Senate permit a freer hand to President Truman should he wish a greater involvement in Southeast Asia?

The Senate was stirred into a "revolt" in 1951 by events taking place outside Indochina. Between 1945 and 1950, there had been numerous examples of spectacular executive initiatives in foreign policy; these included the conferences at Yalta and Potsdam, participation in the United Nations, the Truman Doctrine, the Marshall Plan, the North Atlantic Pact, and the American entry into the Korean war. By the end of 1950, disillusionment with the Cold War, with the mounting casualties in Korea, and the apparent endlessness of that struggle, caused the Republicans to attack the Truman foreign policy, and to raise questions about the growing commitment in Indochina. This would have a major bearing on President Eisenhower's 1954 decision not to rescue the French.

Such an attack had been predictable as early as fall 1949. The *Washington Star* had then observed that "for some time, there had been a restless stirring in the Republican ranks, a rising revolt against the 'me-tooism' which some hold responsible for the succession of GOP disasters at the polls. And there is more than suspicion that some influential Republicans have been playing with the idea of carrying the revolt to the extent of junking the bipartisan foreign policy in the hope that some partisan advantage could be salvaged from the resulting discord."[7] Senator Arthur Vandenberg, the leading Republican exponent of bipartisan foreign policy, saw these developments in more pragmatic terms. "On many counts, I don't like [Truman] better than that they do," he admitted. "But he is the only president and the only commander-in-chief we are going to have for three more critical years."[8] The frustrating Korean War had become a particular irritant to the Republicans.

Powerful elements in the Republican Party had always believed bipartisanship to be wrong as a matter of principle. Earlier in December 1948, former 1936 presidential nominee Alfred Landon had charged that "bipartisan foreign policy has resulted in a blackout—a blackout of intelligent debate in Congress and the press. Both the Republican Party and the Democratic Party have bypassed Congress and party responsibility, with serious consequences."[9]

Historian Norman Graebner charged that in their arrogance, State Department policymakers after 1945 had ignored Congress and had failed to build support which might have defended them from partisan assault. Furthermore, the majority in Congress was convinced that the United States was receiving inadequate assistance from other non–Communist nations in the Cold War struggle.

These criticisms were brought to the surface by the depressing situation in Korea; mounting costs and casualties; limited assistance from the allies, and the confrontation with Communist China all stoked the opposition. Also at this time, the administration had let it be known that it was readying more forces to become part of the projected international army in Europe. All these factors led to the Republican protests in late 1950 and early 1951, focusing upon Truman's policies in both Asia and Europe.

On December 20, 1950, former president Herbert Hoover gave an address which touched off further controversy on U.S. foreign policy. In

II. The Years of Growing Involvement

this address, Hoover suggested the United States should concentrate its defense on its air force and navy and withdraw from Korea if its position there became untenable. The nation should then concentrate on defending Japan and Formosa, drastically limiting the amount of military aid to European nations until they began an all-out effort on their own behalf.[10]

The debate was enhanced when Robert Taft, probably the most influential Republican in the Senate, made a speech in the Senate on January 5, 1951. Taft challenged Truman's constitutional authority to conduct foreign policy as he had been doing until then. This attack signified the beginning of congressional partisan attacks on Truman's foreign policy. Taft attacked appeals for unity as "an attempt to cover up the faults and failures of the administration." He cited as flagrant abuses of executive initiative in foreign policy, the commitment of American troops to Korea without congressional authorization, and the president's proposal to send American troops to Europe, also without congressional authorization. He denied that the North Atlantic Pact had sanctioned or committed the United States to station troops in Europe. "A new policy is being formulated without consulting the Congress or the people," he declared.[11]

One of the core policies of the Truman administration being attacked was the domino theory which was linked to the U.S. position on Indochina. Its advocates believed that if Indochina fell to the Communists, then Burma, Malaya, Thailand, Singapore, possibly Indonesia and the Philippines, would also fall, and even India—and thus the entire balance of power in the world would be altered. It was easy to see why the domino theory could have been accepted then; at the time, guerrilla wars were going on in Burma, the Philippines, Malaya, South Korea, and Indochina.

The issue of troop commitments in Europe was linked to possible troop commitments in Asia. Taft feared that the United States was running the risk of overextending its military capacity in Indochina and elsewhere. He believed that it should avoid troop commitments to such exposed areas as most of continental Asia (including Indochina) and Europe, concentrating instead on Formosa, Japan, North Africa, Spain, the Suez Canal area, Malaya, and Singapore. Sea and air power should be stressed rather than troop commitments. This type of power should be available to assist "those nations which ask for assistance to defend themselves against Communist aggression, to the extent that such power can be successfully and effectively used."[12]

Viewing matters on a worldwide perspective, Taft was also skeptical of Truman's warnings of Russia's drive for world hegemony. Taft had a much more limited view of U.S. foreign policy than President Truman. He doubted that the Russians had the military conquest of the world in mind. "I believe they know it is impossible," he wrote. The policy "on which all Republicans [can] unite [is] one of all-out opposition to the spread of communism, although recognizing that there [is] a limit beyond which we cannot go."[13] His view of Russian aims implied his doubts of the domino theory which was supported by the administration to justify its commitments to such exposed areas as Indochina. Was the United States about to get needlessly bogged down in another Asian quagmire, he wondered?

Despite this growing unease in the Senate, and especially by the Republican Party, during 1950 and 1951, the United States greatly increased its commitment to Indochina with little reaction from the Senate. The year 1950 was one of those pivotal years which determines the course of many of the following years. This was shortly after the Communist victory in China, a worsening of the Cold War, and the beginning of the Korean War. In February of that year, the United States extended diplomatic relations to the regime of Vietnamese Emperor Bao Dai, though it was clearly a client of the French.

Even after the alleged grant of "independence" to Vietnam in 1950, France retained very extensive powers. The transfer of local authority from the French to local officials in Indochina was made with obvious reluctance. In the last years of French rule, there were more French officials in Indochina than there had been British serving throughout India at any time during British rule. France ruled Vietnam through the incompetent "playboy emperor" Bao Dai, as well as local Vietnamese aristocrats who did not challenge the French. The emperor was described by the U.S. ambassador as "not the stuff of which Churchills are made."[14]

The Russian recognition of Ho Chi Minh's government soon afterward signified that the great powers had become involved in the Indochina problem. Russia had never taken the similar step of extending diplomatic relations to the Greek Communists in the post–World War II Greek civil war. Also in May 1950, the United States began to openly aid the French effort in Vietnam for the first time.

The United States was originally reluctant to get too involved in Southeast Asian affairs. Through Secretary of State Dean Acheson, one of the key figures behind the decision to commit the United States to Indochina, the administration now pledged economic and military aid to

II. The Years of Growing Involvement

the French. The State Department had just about decided that Indochina was lost to the Soviet bloc; however, when Acheson was urged to reexamine the problem; he did so and changed his position.

This commitment to Indochina was publicly reported by the *New York Times* in May 1950 when it declared the United States was pledged to the defense of Southeast Asia. It reported: "In an un-deliberate, haphazard way, the United States government is in the process of elaborating what is the equivalent of a "Truman Doctrine" for Southeast Asia. This process, which began slowly and almost unconsciously during the last four months, is now clearly assuming shape as a coordinated strategic policy designed to save one of the world's key areas from being eaten up piecemeal by skillful Communist infiltration. Whether the American people realize it or not, they are now pretty well committed [to the defense

President Harry Truman (*left*) and Secretary of State Dean Acheson, who began the U.S. involvement in Vietnam (Truman Library photograph by Abbie Rowe).

of Southeast Asia]."[15] The commitment was sizable and growing. The United States had agreed to furnish, as an initial investment, $23 million of economic and military aid to help save the three Indochinese states, Vietnam, Laos, and Cambodia. The *Times* added: "It is virtually certain that more will follow if the first amounts are well spent."[16] It also reported that for the first time, the Joint Chiefs of Staff appeared to be concluding that an effort to bolster the Bao Dai regime was worth the gamble—justified by the ever-ominous domino theory.

The Communist attack on South Korea in June 1950 merely accelerated a policy already determined. This policy, outlined in May 1950, by Acheson, declared that France and the Associated States (Vietnam, Cambodia, and Laos), rather than the United States, would assume the major burden of defending Indochina. President Truman's statement on the outbreak of the Korean War included a directive for acceleration in the furnishing of military assistance to the French forces and to her Indochinese allies, and for the dispatch of a military mission to provide close working relations with those forces. Undoubtedly, the administration viewed this action as another flank against the same Communist enemy.

Although there was no immediate opposition to Truman's policy of assistance to Southeast Asia, there was senatorial criticism by the end of the year. Initially, most of the critics centered their fire on the colonial aspect of the French efforts. Later, as the American commitment grew, the critics would stress their opposition to possible American troop intervention in Southeast Asia.

In December 1950, senators Claude Pepper and Wayne Morse argued that the United Nations, rather than the United States, should deal with the problem. Senator Pepper stated that "the time has come when in the larger interests, the United Nations should do with respect to Indochina what it did with respect to Indonesia. It should ask the French and the other forces to come together to the bar of the United Nations and take appropriate steps to see to it that those people have their own country to run in their own way."[17] Senator Wayne Morse concurred, declaring: "If we are going to chart a system of international justice through law, [France] too must submit these great questions to the processes of adjudication."[18] These critics saw the Indochina problem as one of colonialism, and not merely as another front in the worldwide struggle against the Communist conspiracy.

These criticisms were brought to the surface by the depressing situ-

II. The Years of Growing Involvement

ation in Korea. Mounting costs and casualties, limited assistance from the Allies, and the confrontation with Communist China all stoked the opposition. Also at this time, the administration had let it be known that it was readying more forces to become part of the projected international army in Europe. These factors led to the growing Republican unease toward Truman's policies in both Asia and Europe.

One of the strongest rebuttals to Taft's concerns of U.S. overcommitments around the world came from Senator Tom Connelly, the chairman of the Foreign Relations Committee. He reiterated the domino theory as a justification for the Indochina commitments, an idea which Taft had attacked. There were also other reasons to back France in Vietnam. Connelly believed that a French victory would release French manpower and resources for use in the North Atlantic Treaty Organization (NATO) alliance.[19]

During the following year, the failure of the French to improve their military situation and the growing American commitment intensified the debate in the Senate. Taft reaffirmed his earlier position that material aid, but not American troops, should be extended to the French.

Senator Hugh Butler specifically linked the Indochina commitments to the debate over the Senate's foreign policy prerogatives. Fearing that Truman had organized another "Korean adventure," Butler expressed concern over the bypassing of the constitutional "advise and consent" powers of the Senate. He regarded any agreements committing American troops to the war in Indochina as having the legal status of a treaty, requiring consent by two-thirds of the Senate. Therefore, he declared: "If the president has made any such agreement, it is null and void. It

Senator Robert Taft, an early critic of U.S. involvement in Vietnam (U.S. Senate Historical Office).

does not commit the United States to any action unless and until (the president) has received the advice and consent of two-thirds of the Senate."[20] The senator then concluded that "the people of America are entitled to have a say in the matter through their elected representatives before they are called upon to do battle on behalf of French imperial interests in distant Asia."[21] Butler acted upon his indignation by co-sponsoring a resolution with eighteen other senators, calling upon the president to make a full disclosure of the results of his recently concluded conferences with Prime Minister Churchill and other officials of the British government on this matter.

Despite Butler's attack, the commitment to Indochina grew steadily. The previous September, the United States had signed an agreement with Vietnam for direct economic assistance. In March 1952, Defense Secretary Robert Lovett suggested the possibility of American intervention in Indochina, although in concert with other United Nations forces. In July, the United States legation in Saigon was raised to Embassy status, and the Vietnamese Embassy was established in Washington, D.C.

Under the new Eisenhower administration, the American commitment to Indochina continued to escalate, despite concerns expressed by the Senate. Eisenhower had campaigned in 1952 to halt further Communist expansion. In January 1953, the administration announced through Senator Mike Mansfield, its intention to put Indochina on equal footing with Korea as an area of military crisis. (Although a leading critic of escalation in the 1960s, Senator Mansfield ironically was the earliest and most persistent backer on the Foreign Relations Committee for heavy aid to the French, short of involvement of United States troops, against the Communist-led rebels in Indochina.) In February, the *New York Times* reported that the administration was considering a major contribution in money and munitions to help the French war effort. Testifying before the Senate Foreign Relations Committee in April, Secretary of State John Foster Dulles described Southeast Asia as "the world's most dangerous spot." Senior members of the committee took a worried view of the outlook in Indochina. They feared the Eisenhower administration had already decided to put much more emphasis on military assistance to Asia.

Secretary Dulles had intimated that the Indochinese situation was perhaps even more dangerous than the Korean problem. Dulles claimed that the fall-out from a defeat in Indochina would be much harder to con-

II. The Years of Growing Involvement

tain than from Korea since it was not as isolated as the Korean peninsula. The stakes could be very high if the French were defeated in Indochina.

By May 1953, the Indochina issue was widely debated in the Senate for the first time. In this debate, the Senate stressed the two themes of opposition to French colonialism and American intervention. The latter possibility grew ever more likely as the French position failed to improve. On May 3, Senator Leverett Saltonstall, chairman of the Senate Armed Services Committee, declared his opposition to dispatching troops to Southeast Asia. "We can spread our butter too thin," he stated. "If we are going to spread ourselves all over the world where people can't help themselves, we're not going to have much left in this country."[22]

There were also advocates for a more aggressive U.S. position. Senator William Knowland, a longtime "hawk" on foreign policy, supported the use of American air and naval power in Asia, but refrained from urging that American troops be sent to Vietnam. Senator Paul Douglas was an even more unwavering "hawk"; his position was consistent in 1953, 1954, and after 1964. In May 1953, he criticized the Eisenhower administration for acting less promptly and effectively with the Indochina crisis that had former President Truman in the Korean crisis in 1950.

By June, as the French military position failed to improve, the opponents of a direct military commitment became more vocal in the Senate. Senator Guy Gillette declared: "If [the administration policy] is committing the United States to the war in Indochina, I repudiate it. I refuse to be committed."[23] He also cautioned against appropriating excessive funds for the administration's Indochina policy. A debate had broken out at this time over a proposed cut in funds for Indochina from $400 million to $300 million. In supporting the measure, Gillette stated: "I would ... abdicate my responsibility by turning over a blank check to the president."[24]

Senator Ralph Flanders focused his criticism on France's failure to grant independence to Indochina. He queried: "Why should we not suggest to the French government ... that it give assurance to the promise of independence for Cambodia and Laos, and thereby undermine the strength of the opposition which the French are meeting in Vietnam at the present time?"[25] He added that such a step would also "relieve us of some of the tremendous undertakings into which we may be drawn willy-nilly by our own unwillingness to use imagination and courage in this particular situation."[26]

Senators John Kennedy and Ralph Potter also stressed this theme of independence for Indochina. Kennedy asserted: "I believe it is of the utmost importance at a time when the United States is committing itself deeper and deeper into Indochina, that our influence and prestige with the French be used to promote the independence and well-being of the people of the Associated States. If we do so, not only will the prospect of victory be substantially enhanced, but the position of the United States, France, and of the whole Western alliance will be materially advanced in Asia."[27]

Although he staunchly advocated independence for Vietnam, Kennedy did not take the bold position of urging a rapprochement with Ho Chi Minh. He stated on the Senate floor on June 30, 1953:

> Many people argue that in 1945, Ho Chi Minh was right for "Titoism" [an independent version of communism] if the French had been willing to grant him sufficient political concessions. It is difficult to be convinced of this, although it is true that in November 1945, he did dissolve the Indochinese Communist Party and took similar conciliatory steps to gain the support of a majority of the people. But his record as a leading and active world Communist figure argues against this theory of "Titoism," and the seizure of control by the Communists in China at a later date would have placed him in the most difficult position if he had attempted to break his ties with Moscow.[28]

Supporting Kennedy's focus on independence, Senator Potter introduced a resolution stating that "the Congress recognizes the desire for freedom, and independence, and self-government's of the peoples of the Associated States of Laos, Cambodia, and Vietnam, and hope the governments of France will encourage and make preparation for the independence, self-government, and freedom of these Associated States at a time determined and agreed by the governments of these Associated States of the government of France."[29]

Other senators joined in the rising tide of criticism. Also supporting independence for Vietnam, Senator Barry Goldwater introduced an amendment to condition and reduce the aid level in the Mutual Security Act. It stated that "no such expenditure shall be made until the government of France gives satisfactorily assurance to the president of the United States that an immediate declaration will be made to the people of the Associated States, setting a target date for adoption of a constitution for such states and for the establishment of their complete independence."[30] The senator explained his amendments as saying to France: "If we give you this money, we expect you to do something in return for it because as surely as day follows night, our boys will follow this $400 million [aid appropriation]."[31]

II. The Years of Growing Involvement

The way to stop this, he added, was to ask France to grant independence and the right of freedom to these people "who have fought so long for their independence and freedom." Since France was unwilling to continue the war if it meant the loss of its colonies, the Goldwater "solution" could not be enacted.

Senators Flanders and Everett Dirksen attacked the American policy toward Indochina outright. Flanders denounced the aid appropriation bill as a "stop-gap measure," and attacked American policy as "feeble and vacillating." He pledged he would not vote for any such aid bills in the future unless the American policy was changed. Senator Dirksen queried why the United States, after delivering such vast amounts of aid to the French, could not pressure that government into a target date for independence, for a constitution, and for freedom.

The amendment to cut $100 million from the French aid appropriation was defeated, partly because of the strong opposition of Senator Mansfield. The senator called Southeast Asia the key to Asia whose loss would be a "great catastrophe." He stated: "I do not want American boys sent to Indochina, but I am afraid that a possible consequence we face, if this aid is cut, is a withdrawal from Indochina by the French."[32] He further added that there was a "good possibility" of victory in Indochina within a period of two years if American aid were not cut. Other senators added that the aid cuts would cause the French to lose heart in their efforts, and that any slackening of this effort would cause the Chinese Communists to step up their own efforts in Southeast Asia. Consequently, the pro-administration forces carried the day, and the aid cut was restored.

Senator Ralph Flanders, who warned against U.S. involvement in Vietnam in the late 1940s (U.S. Senate Historical Office).

Bystanders to the Vietnam War

Toward the end of 1953, the momentum clearly was shifting in favor of the commitment to Indochina, as the French position continued to decline. At the governors' conference in August, President Eisenhower reiterated the domino theory to justify his Southeast Asian policy. In September, Secretary Dulles added that the American people had not been sufficiently appreciative of the French sacrifices.

At this time, senators Knowland and Mansfield as well as Vice President Nixon made visits to this area and afterward expressed support for halting Communist expansion in Indochina. Repeating his usual hard line, Knowland declared he was convinced that the United States never would stand by unconcerned in the face of a new Communist aggression, including a Chinese invasion of Indochina. Mansfield called recognition of the aspirations of the Indochinese states as well as aid by the United States the key to victory. He attributed Ho Chi Minh's great popularity, and the consequent French quagmire, to the widespread desire for independence from foreign control. Vice President Nixon similarly stressed the importance of a vigorous American commitment and the necessity of victory. He told the French that "it is impossible to lay down arms until victory is completely won." There was obviously considerable support for halting communism in Asia but no consensus on a precise strategy.

There were also other political pressures on the administration of a different nature which could not be ignored in consideration of the Indochina policy, arising from the very controversial Bricker amendment. First introduced in 1952, this amendment would limit the president's power to negotiate treaties without prior consultation with the Congress. This amendment expressed the widely shared resentment (partic-

Senator William Knowland, one of the leading "hawks" in the 1950s, who called for a strong commitment to halt Communist expansion in Asia (U.S. Senate Historical Office).

II. The Years of Growing Involvement

ularly among Republican congressmen) that Roosevelt and Truman had abused executive authority in negotiating treaties. The Bricker amendment supposedly would restore the Constitution to a form in which the Congress would be almost the equal of the president in the execution of foreign policy.

Eisenhower was strongly opposed to the Bricker amendment which he regarded as a "thorn in our side." During a cabinet discussion of the measure, he cried out in anguish: "I'm so sick of this, I could scream. The whole damn thing is senseless and plain damaging to the prestige of the United States. We talk about the French not being able to govern themselves—and we sit here wrestling with the Bricker amendment."[33]

Congressional debate on the amendment began in 1954. After clearing the Senate Judiciary Committee, the bill reached the Senate floor on January 20. Five days later, President Eisenhower wrote to the Senate Majority Leader William Knowland, objecting to the Bricker amendment as being unduly restrictive of the president's powers. "Adoption [of the amendment] would be notice to our friends as well as our enemies abroad that our country intends to withdraw from its leadership in world affairs."[34]

Eisenhower Republicans, with the support of Democratic votes, were ultimately able to defeat the measure in the Senate. But the strength of the "Brickerites" served as a warning to the executive not to ignore the views of the principal Republican leaders in Congress in the creation of future policy, including the Indochina problem. The Eisenhower administration was compelled to a substantial degree, to assure Congress that its leaders would be consulted frequently on serious matters such as the commitment of combat troops in crisis areas. This would later have an important bearing upon the president's handling of the 1954 Indochina crisis.

Eisenhower's view of the presidency complemented this resurgence in congressional initiative. He interpreted his role as chief executive differently from Roosevelt and Truman. He would not overly pressure the Senate, as his predecessors had often done, to go along with his policies. "I am not one of the desk-pounding types that likes to stick out his jaw and look like he is bossing the show," he said at a news conference. "I don't think it is the function of the president of the United States to punish anybody from voting as he likes."[35]

Eisenhower did not believe in acting dictatorial to Congress. He stated: "You do not lead by hitting people over the head.... You don't lead a man by yelling at him in public or forcing him to say publicly: 'yes, it's true—I've been voting like a damn fool ever since I came to Congress 20 years ago.'"[36] He described leadership as persuasion, conciliation, education, and patience. "That's the only kind of leadership I know—or believe in—or will practice."[37] Furthermore, during his campaign for the presidency in 1952, Eisenhower had at times been critical of Truman's method of involvement in the war in Korea. According to historian Wilfred Binkley, this came to have a "peculiar effect" on his relations with Congress during his presidency.[38]

This "effect" would be manifested in 1954 when Eisenhower was forced to make a vital decision: should the French be rescued by direct American intervention? By the end of 1953, despite increasing Senate opposition and a series of abortive attempts to influence the president's policy, the United States had steadily increased its commitment to Indochina. Yet, because of Eisenhower's personal views and the strong senatorial pressure on him, any decision to commit American troops to aid the French would necessitate winning approval of the Senate. Another "Korean adventure," launched solely by the president, without consulting Congress, would not be repeated.

III

The Decision Not to Intervene

The Indochina crisis of 1954 demonstrated the Senate's concerns over being neglected as the nation moved toward another "Korea." After four years of assisting the French in Indochina, the United States was confronted with a vital decision in the spring of 1954. The deteriorating French position, dramatized by the struggle at Dien Bien Phu, necessitated a change in American policy. The Eisenhower administration seemed to be moving toward unilateral intervention when strong opposition from the Senate led it to be more deliberate. The president's strong personal doubts, reinforced by the Senate's often expressed opposition as well as equally strong opposition from the British, ultimately led him to drop the idea of intervention.

With the Vietnam war not going well, in May 1953, France appointed General Henri Navarre as its new commander, and offered a new strategy to win the war. The so-called Navarre Plan called for a much larger French force, with a strategy for a major offensive in northern Vietnam instead of a host of scattered operations. It also included vague references to Vietnamese independence as well as more reliance on the native Vietnamese forces. Although not overly optimistic, the United States agreed to finance the expanded French operations with an additional $400 million. Privately, the Eisenhower administration believed the new strategy to be a "long shot."

The upcoming battle of Dien Bien Phu would later have an extremely important effect on the war. Over Secretary Dulles' vigorous opposition in early 1954, France agreed to place Indochina on the agenda of an East-West conference scheduled to meet in Geneva to consider Asian problems. France was hoping a significant victory under the aggressive Navarre Plan would help gain them a favorable outcome at the conference.

Bystanders to the Vietnam War

In early 1954, both the French and the Vietnamese Communists committed vast forces to the remote area of Dien Bien Phu in the northwest corner of Vietnam. Navarre's strategy was to lure the Vietminh into a major battle where he could deliver a decisive blow. Navarre, however, now found 12,000 of his elite forces trapped in a fortress in a far corner of Vietnam. Rather than withdraw to a more secure area, he decided to remain. The French would soon find themselves surrounded by 48,000 Vietcong troops.

On March 13, the Communists launched an all-out attack. The heavy Vietminh guns quickly knocked out the airfield, making resupply impossible except by parachute drop and leaving the garrison of 12,000 men isolated and vulnerable. The Eisenhower administration now faced a serious crisis, and weighed how it might save the French from a devastating defeat. This would prove to be a defining moment in the Indochina crisis.

In the first few months of 1954, the administration had launched a set of trial balloons to test Congress' response to a more aggressive policy in Indochina. Each time, the U.S. Senate registered opposition. The first test came in early February when the administration decided, without consulting Congress, to send 200 plane technicians to assist the French. The Senate's response was immediate and harshly critical. Typical was the comment by Senator Mansfield who declared that the situation in Indochina could not be allowed to drift any longer. Speaking for the administration, however, Senator Knowland attempted to still criticism by giving "categorical assurances" that this move did not indicate an intent to send ground troops to Asia.

Other senators were clearly concerned over the possibility of U.S. involvement in the Vietnamese war. Senator John Stennis called the administration's move a dangerous step that might lead to direct intervention. He insisted that the Americans be returned home at the earliest possible date, and expressed concern that the United States would become directly involved if the technicians were attacked or captured. Senator Richard Russell deemed the administration's action an "unnecessary risk." Fearing another "Korea," Senator Walter George and other Democrats said this action was a "mistake" that could lead the United States into piecemeal participation in the Indochina war.

The Senate's criticism evolved into a public debate over the executive's willingness to join the war in Indochina. In order to quell the Senate's

III. The Decision Not to Intervene

Senator John Stennis, an early critic of possible U.S. involvement in the French Vietnam War in 1954 (U.S. Senate Historical Office).

uneasiness, President Eisenhower asserted at his press conference on February 10 that he "could not conceive of no greater tragedy than for the United States to become involved in an all-out war in Indochina." He added that no one could be more bitterly opposed to such a development than he. Every move authorized by him, said the president, was calculated, "so far as is humanly possible, to make certain that the United States did not get involved in a hot war in the Indochina region."[1]

Several days later, the Senate Foreign Relations Committee heard testimony from Assistant Secretary of State Walter Bedell Smith and from the head of the Joint Chiefs of Staff, Admiral William Radford, on this matter. One reason for the meeting had been the committee's Democratic members' complaints that the administration had bypassed them in deciding to support the French with additional Air Force technicians.

Furthermore, committee members were said to be alarmed over the possibility of United States involvement in the war in Southeast Asia. The meeting was also expected to attempt to discover precisely what the government's "New Look" defense strategy demanded, where Congress' rights fitted into this strategy, and how it was to be used in places such as Indochina. (The "New Look" strategy was an emphasis on air power, with a consequent reduction in the number of ground troops, in an attempt to cut defense spending.) Some of the senators were criticizing the administration for relying on a policy they felt didn't really apply to the Communist tactic of the "proxy war." Others were criticizing the administration for getting too involved in Indochina without telling Congress what it was doing. Clearly there was a growing unease in Congress about a possible new Asian war.

The committee meeting attempted to deal with these questions. At the hearings, Assistant Secretary of State Walter Bedell Smith promised to see that no major moves would be made in the future without prior consultation on Capitol Hill. In the event that Communist China intervened in the Indochina war or if the military situation deteriorated seriously, Smith and Radford said the matter would then have to be submitted to Congress. Smith also declared there was no intention of putting United States ground troops in Indochina.

Three weeks later, Senator Stennis reopened the Indochina debate by reissuing his warning that the United States was moving closer toward active involvement in Asia. His concern was prompted by reports that the Vietminh planned to attack every area where American personnel were working. He also put in the *Congressional Record* a letter to Defense Secretary Charles Wilson, urging the immediate withdrawal of all American forces. He renewed his earlier request that the Air Force technicians be withdrawn saying, "For all the good they do, the risk is too great."[2]

At his news conference the following day, this mounting concern over the drift toward another Asian war and, in particular, strong criticism by 1952 Democratic presidential nominee Adlai Stevenson, led President Eisenhower to reopen the debate over the executive's war-making powers The president promised not to involve the United States in war without a declaration of war by Congress. By this statement, the president seemed to modify the policy of "instant retaliation" previously announced by Dulles. Eisenhower also seemed to commit himself to the requirement of a declaration of war by Congress, regardless of the circumstances in the future or whether Congress was in session at the time of the crisis.

Not willing to bind the administration's diplomatic and military options, Eisenhower and Dulles modified this rigid promise in the following week. Dulles stated that the United States would respond to a sudden attack on the United States or a Communist Chinese attack in Indochina, even if Congress were not in session. Soon afterward, Eisenhower again modified his position on retaliation. If the interests of the nation were threatened, the president would make a common sense judgment of the situation. If the threat were dire, he would commit the armed forces and then consult Congress. But if time permitted, he would seek a declaration

III. The Decision Not to Intervene

of war by Congress before acting. During the turbulent days of April, Eisenhower made this last statement the keynote of his policy.

To clarify this vital issue even further, the Senate Foreign Relations Committee further questioned Secretary Dulles. Citing circumstances which might require an immediate response, Dulles declined to give any promise that President Eisenhower would consult with Congress before committing the United States to war. "If time permits, Congress, of course, should share the responsibility," he stated.[3]

This debate over the president's war-making initiative, coming at a time when the Senate was fearful of another "Korea," was no mere semantical question. As the battle of Dien Bien Phu intensified, the administration showed an increasing concern over the events in Southeast Asia. On March 25, President Eisenhower declared that the freedom of all Southeast Asia was of "transcendent importance" to the entire free world. On March 28th, the administration's foreign policy spokesman in the Senate, Alexander Wiley, declared that if France did not continue to "play ball," the West would be in a "terrible fix."[4]

On the following night, Dulles solemnly declared that Communist domination of Indochina and Southeast Asia "would be a grave threat to the whole free world community." He added: "That possibility should not be passively accepted and should be met by unified action."[5] Dulles's words implied the possibility of further steps. He claimed that the united action he proposed might involve risks, but these would be far less than those to be faced if the United States was not resolute.

The administration had clearly launched a set of trial balloons to test the Congress and public opinion on the possibility of intervening in Indochina. It now felt that the French and the Associated States could not win the war by themselves, and that while they would need the help of the United States, public opinion had not been prepared for American intervention. The administration was attempting to make clear to everybody, including the American people, that this region would not be allowed to slip away to the Communists.

On Capitol Hill, the response to the possibility of United States intervention was less than enthusiastic—predictable inasmuch as 1954 was an election year and only one year removed from the end of the Korean War. In the Senate, there were many complaints concerning the lack of adequate information. Senator Ralph Watkins stated, "It is the duty of the president to advise the Congress so that Congress can grant him, under its Constitutional power, authority to go ahead." He added his hope that "the president will not follow the example of President Truman and take action without consulting Congress."[6] Senator Stennis added that "while no one was being dishonest, members of the Armed Services Committee were not getting enough information upon which to base a judgment."[7] Several senior Democrats in the Senate disclosed that they had not even been consulted by Dulles in advance of his speech.

Congressional leaders clearly indicated their ideas of united action to Dulles and the administration at a secret, top-level meeting held on April 3. On that day, Dulles, Radford, and several aides met with eight congressional leaders. Dulles said the president wanted to take up with them legislative action short of a declaration of war or the use of ground troops. The secretary stated that if Congress would permit the president to use air and naval power, then a way could be found to prevent a broadening of the conflict. Admiral Radford suggested that if Congress passed a joint resolution giving the president general power to act, it would be possible with only a single airstrike, to relieve the embattled fortress of Dien Bien Phu, then under siege for three months. The possibility of using low-yield nuclear weapons was also discussed.

The congressional leaders then asked several pointed questions. Radford was asked if such a strike would be an act of war. Also, if such a strike did not succeed, would the United States then follow it up with U.S. ground troops? Radford was forced to confess that none of the other Joint Chiefs of Staff agreed with him on the air strike. (One of the Joint Chiefs, General Nathan Twining, said he might back the plan but only subject to certain conditions that the French would probably not support.) Dulles was asked why he did not go to the United Nations. The secretary was also forced to admit that none of the other allies had lined up with the United States on this strategy. The congressional leaders suggested that he should first obtain agreement from the allies before asking Congress to take any action, and the meeting broke up on this note.

On April 6, a significant speech by Senator John Kennedy helped shift the focal point of the Indochina debate to the Senate floor. Calling on the administration to tell the American people the "blunt truths" about Indochina, Kennedy stressed the vital significance of ensuring the immediate independence of the people of that region. Otherwise, Kennedy believed that "no amount of American military assistance could conquer an enemy which was everywhere and at the same time nowhere,

III. The Decision Not to Intervene

an enemy of the people which had the sympathy and covert support of the people."[8]

On the same day, remarks by other senators reaffirmed those conditions outlined by the congressional leaders in their meeting with administration officials on April 3; independence for the Indochinese peoples, a continued military effort by the French, and assistance from our European allies and various Asian governments. Senator John Sherman Cooper observed that these conditions were actually impossible to fulfill in the immediate future, and would have made Senate approval of intervention impossible.

In that Senate debate, the various viewpoints in the Senate on intervention were revealed. Senators Knowland and Henry Jackson took a relatively aggressive position. Knowland stressed that the United States' allies be ready to contribute their share of military strength should the United States and the free world be forced to fight in Southeast Asia. Senator Jackson urged the president to come before Congress to say what he would require in the way of backing, promising the Democrats would not be found unwilling to help.

On the other hand, one voice in total opposition in all circumstances of possible American intervention was that of Senator Everett Dirkson. The Illinois senator announced that he was opposed to any such course, contending that United States troops were not actually needed. In a contrary point of view, Senator Stennis spoke for the majority opinion when he declared that Congress might have to agree to intervention—if America's allies joined in this move, and only if absolutely necessary, and according to the Senate's previously stated conditions.

Despite the general reluctance of the Senate to support intervention, the administration seemed to be moving toward committing American troops to Asia. Secretary Dulles flew to Europe, attempting to create the allied coalition on which the Senate was insisting as a precondition for its assent. At a news conference on April 8, President Eisenhower stated the problem in its most gloomy aspect. He claimed a Communist conquest of Indochina would set off throughout Asia a chain reaction for the free world, a reference to the falling domino theory. Yet he declined to say at this time whether the United States would seek collective action or as a last resort, go it alone to save Indochina.

By this time, the intervention debate in the Senate was taking on somewhat of a partisan aspect. The Republicans sought to ensure that if the United States did get involved, there would not be a repetition of Korea where the allies committed only token forces and assistance. Accordingly, much of the president's Republican support in the Senate came in the form of a warning that United States foreign aid should be withdrawn from those governments that refuse to join the common effort. One of the leaders of this group was Senator Styles Bridges, chairman of the Appropriations Committee. Responding to Democratic criticism that such a policy was "economic blackmail," Bridges declared: "Certainly a nation that has given over $105 billion to help other countries of the world build up their economies has every right to expect full cooperation from the participating nations."[9]

Taking a different position, the Democrats stressed the importance of granting full independence for the three Associated States; this was designed to remove the colonial taint from the American Southeast Asia policy. A typical example came from Senator Estes Kefauver's position to reassure the people of Indochina that they would win their freedom as they resisted communism. The United States, he said, might be able to avoid "another Korea" by firmly supporting freedom and placing the problem before the United Nations. "Let us return to the great American tradition and support that very natural desire by demonstrating that we want the states of Indochina to be free," he urged.[10]

The French position on Indochina complicated the situation for the United States. France was reluctant to offer independence to Indochina, and wished the United States to serve as the junior partner in the war. The United States would supply materials, but France would retain primary authority on military decisions in the region. Unwilling to agree and critical of France's military efforts, the United States claimed the French had "botched" the war. The French had failed to recruit adequate numbers of local Vietnamese to fight. They also had refused to agree to genuine independence, thus removing the taint of colonialism.

It was difficult for the United States to persuade France to change its policies. Unless the United States continued to give France a virtual free hand, hopefully permitting some sort of settlement agreeable to France, it threatened not to join the European Defense Community, the military arm of NATO. As with its dealings with Vietnamese leader Ngo Dinh Diem in the following years, the United States could pressure its ally only to a limited degree.

While the Senate debate was attempting to clarify conditions under

III. The Decision Not to Intervene

which intervention might be possible, the administration launched another trial balloon on April 16—in the form of a speech by Vice President Richard Nixon. With remarkable candor, he declared that if France stopped fighting in Indochina and if the situation demanded it, the United States would have to intervene with combat troops. As a leader of the free world, the United States could not afford another retreat in Asia. His theme was to fight now or have to fight later.[11]

Nixon's speech was followed by demands in the Senate from both sides of the aisle for a clarification of the government's policy. Senator Hubert Humphrey lamented that the Democrats had to get administration policy by reading the newspapers. Senator Ralph Flanders, a strong supporter of the president, called upon the chief executive to tell the world in candid fashion what the administration policy was. The Senate apparently feared that the United States was on the verge of making the final commitment to the war in Southeast Asia.

Yet events taking place outside the capitol helped ensure that these fears would go unrealized. Dulles's efforts to organize the united front to rescue Dien Bien Phu had been rebuffed by the British, and he was so informed on April 18. The next day, in blunt terms, Churchill told Eisenhower: "If we didn't fight for India, why would we fight for France's colony in Indochina?"[12] Eisenhower's long personal letter to Churchill, urging support for intervention, had failed. Churchill did not believe that defeat in Vietnam would doom all of Southeast Asia, questioning the basic premise of the domino theory. Dulles, after meeting with President Eisenhower soon afterward, told reporters it was unlikely that American troops would be sent to Indochina. Britain's position was to give negotiations a chance. Military action would doom the chances for a peaceful solution, and it was better to await the outcome of the meetings taking place in Geneva.

Though the prospects for United States intervention were greatly reduced by this time, the administration apparently had not definitely abandoned the idea. In late April, Dulles flew to Paris and London in another attempt to create an allied coalition, and was again unsuccessful.

The administration's agreement to transport French Union troops to Indochina served as another trial balloon, and met with a negative reaction from Congress. This move was roundly criticized by the Senate, which continued to be cool to each escalation of the American involvement. Stennis, who earlier opposed the sending of United States technicians, said the airlift was "just another step closer to war." Even a leading

Bystanders to the Vietnam War

President Dwight Eisenhower (left) and Secretary of State John Foster Dulles, who avoided a war but presided over the growing U.S. involvement in Vietnam during the 1950s (U.S. State Department Office of the Historian).

Republican defender of the move, Senator Homer Ferguson, carefully reiterated his continued opposition to putting American troops in Indochina.

By late April, the Senate was clearly making its opposition to intervention more vocal. In a reversal of the domino theory, Mansfield stated the terrible "dominoes" which would fall if the United States did intervene. Such a move, he said, would require "a goodly number" of American divisions, was likely to draw Communist China into the war, and might even bring the Soviet Union into conflict with the United States. Senator Edwin Johnson attacked the proposal for American intervention as "the most foolhardy venture in all American history." Johnson predicted the United States armed intervention "would mean a minimum of 500,000 American casualties and a very minimum of $500 billion of borrowed money." He added that such a war could last as long as ten years.[13] When Undersec-

III. The Decision Not to Intervene

retary Smith raised the question of unilateral American military action to a group of Congressional leaders and met strong opposition, the administration could not have been surprised.

Toward the end of April, the administration had clearly reached the decision not to intervene and, in a reversal of the previous few weeks, attempted to prepare public opinion for nonintervention. At a White House meeting with legislative leaders on April 26, the president stated that the United States is not going to "carry the rest of the world on its back," and that he had no intention of sending in American forces independently. Three days later, he publicly declared that he was trying to steer a course between the "unattainable" (complete victory) and the "unacceptable" (a Communist takeover of all of Southeast Asia).

Eisenhower was not unaware of various historical parallels when he told several legislative leaders on April 26 that he would not intervene at Dien Bien Phu. Senator Knowland had cautioned him that "if we don't offer to do something, [critics] will say we are not facing up to the situation." "Well, they've said that before," Eisenhower stated. "They said it about the Democrats during the Chinese situation during the forties. And they said it about [Secretary of State] Henry Stimson when the Japanese invaded Manchuria in the early thirties." Nor did Eisenhower see fit to apply the 1938 Munich "appeasement" analogy to Indochina.

It became administration policy at this time to deemphasize the importance of Indochina to the political future of Southeast Asia. Vice President Nixon, in a reversal of his April 16 speech, stressed the administration's desire to avoid intervention. In early May, Secretary Dulles indicated that the United States had virtually abandoned all hope of effective united action in Vietnam, and that he was seeking a collective security system designed to seal off and protect Laos and Cambodia. On June 3, Defense Secretary Wilson gave the impression to the press that armed intervention was scarcely imminent. Eight days later, the president said, "as of the moment" he had no plans to request congressional standby authority for action in Indochina.

The question of the United States intervening specifically to rescue the beleaguered fortress was decided earlier on May 7 when the French surrendered after fifty-five days of resistance. Although only five percent of their troops in the country were defeated at Dien Bien Phu, France had lost the will to fight. The battle of Dien Bien Phu was called "the most spectacular victory by a colony against the colonial power in the twentieth century."[14] Whether an American intervention could have saved the French fortress would remain unanswered. Even the question whether the Congress would have consented to such an intervention had always been very questionable.

Eisenhower never appealed to the Senate for a resolution backing intervention. On May 29, Senator Kennedy stated that if the president had requested congressional authorization to intervene at that time, he might have been refused.[15] Yet that same month, when Chalmers Roberts, a respected Washington reporter, surveyed congressional leaders on this point, he reached a different conclusion. He declared that if the president had gone before Congress and stated the necessity for intervention, he probably would have received congressional authorization.[16] Another leading reporter seconded Chalmers' conclusion. During the crisis period, and until the fall of Dien Bien Phu, William S. White, the *New York Times* Washington correspondent, said that if the president wanted the authority to intervene, he could have mustered sufficient support in Congress.[17]

The most important factor behind American non-intervention in Vietnam, however, lay with President Eisenhower's inner doubts. Throughout the crisis period, Eisenhower harbored strong reservations about intervening in Southeast Asia. One of these concerned the political nature of the struggle. In his memoirs, he wrote: "The enemy had much popular sympathy, and many civilians aided them by providing both shelter and information. The French still had sufficient forces to win if they could induce the regular Vietnamese soldiers to fight vigorously with them and the populace to support them. But guerrilla warfare cannot work two ways; normally only one side can enjoy reliable citizen help."[18] Eisenhower was convinced that the French could not win the war because the internal political situation in Vietnam had severely weakened their military position.

One of the most decisive factors in convincing Eisenhower that American intervention to rescue the floundering French effort would either be fruitless or too costly was the Ridgway report which reached the president sometime before the fall of Dien Bien Phu on May 7. (General Matthew Ridgway had succeeded MacArthur as the U.S. commander in Korea in 1951.) The report concluded that the United States, had it decided upon involvement, would have faced a major military commitment with the anticipated losses on a scale far greater than had been incurred in Korea. The report also stated that many more combat divisions would have been

III. The Decision Not to Intervene

required than were available under the "New Look" policy. General Ridgway believed that this report "played a considerable, perhaps decisive, role in persuading our government not to embark on that adventure."[19]

Regarding a proposed air raid on Dien Bien Phu, the president had doubts as to its military effectiveness. Some time afterward, he commented: "Well, I couldn't think of anything probably less effective than in a great big jungle area and with the besieged fortress, trying to relieve it with air power. I just can't see how this could have been done unless you were willing to use weapons that could have destroyed the jungles all around the area for miles and that would what probably destroyed Dien Bien Phu itself, and that would've been that."[20] Viewed on a wider scale, Eisenhower had doubts as to the value of Indochina to the security of the United States. James Reston, a writer for the *New York Times*, concluded that Eisenhower, like his Republican predecessors, Herbert Hoover and Theodore Roosevelt, "is hard to convince that United States interests in the Orient are worth a war."[21] He added that the president believed it was a mistake for the United States to dispatch troops to local conflicts around the world. Confirming Reston's views, Eisenhower declared that he "could conceive of no greater disadvantage to America than to be employing its own ground forces, and any other kind of forces, in great numbers around the world, meeting each little situation as it arises. What we are trying to do is to make our friends strong enough to take care of local situations by themselves."[22]

Even had he felt that Indochina had great military value to American security, other factors would have tended to persuade the president not to intervene. One of his leading advisers, presidential aide Sherman Adams observed: "Having avoided one total war with Communist China the year before in Korea when he had the United Nations support, Eisenhower was in no mood to provoke another one in Indochina by going it alone in a military action without the British and other Western allies."[23] Doubtless, Eisenhower remembered his role as head of the great wartime Western coalition in Europe, and was leery of engaging in military ventures without allies.

In the end, the decision not to intervene was a personal decision rather than one forced upon the president by the Senate's reservations or the British opposition. The administration's bellicose position through April was partly designed to prevent Communist China and Russia from escalating their assistance to the Communist rebels in Indochina. It was also directed toward bolstering the French morale in their deteriorating military effort. Furthermore, the administration wished to keep a stiff posture, with an eye toward the upcoming Geneva conference where the problem would have to be resolved by nonmilitary means. By creating a crisis atmosphere, Eisenhower also facilitated Dulles' efforts toward the creation of what later became known as the Southeast Asia Treaty Organization (SEATO).

IV

The Creation of the Southeast Asia Treaty Organization

The SEATO agreement, like all else pertaining to the Vietnam quagmire, had a controversial history. The possibility of such a pact had been discussed as early as 1951, but not until the United States was on the brink of intervening in the Indochina war in 1954 was the pact negotiated. Originally it was designed to threaten and, if necessary, to expedite American intervention, and later to tie the United States closer to Indochina, particularly South Vietnam. Principally, the executive branch seized the initiative in the creation of SEATO. The Senate did play a vital role, however, in encouraging the executive to create SEATO and in ultimately defining its limited applicability.

The origin of SEATO predated the 1954 crisis which eventually brought it into existence. Its inception was aided by the passage of the Vandenberg Resolution of June 1948, which proposed that the United States give military aid to defensive alliances of free nations. Ever since both the Australia, New Zealand, and United States Security Pact (ANZUS), and the Philippine Treaty negotiations were initiated in 1950, American policy aimed at eventually creating a more comprehensive system of regional security in the Pacific area. At this time, however, the United States refused to invite either Great Britain or France to become parties to these treaties because to do so would have involved their colonies in Malaya and Indochina, which were already faced with Communist insurrection. The United States strategy was to avoid commitments, with the exception of obligations under the United Nations charter, on the mainland of Asia that might involve American ground troops.

The Eisenhower administration, like its predecessor, took a positive view towards Far Eastern collective defense arrangements. On March 16, 1953, President Eisenhower stated in a speech: "The free world knows that aggressions in Korea and Southeast Asia are threats to the whole free community to be met only through united action."[1] Yet the Southeast Asia pact idea might well have been abandoned had not the situation suddenly worsened in Indochina, and thereby stimulated the American desire for a united front in this area. The United States was fearful of the consequences of a diplomatic solution in Vietnam, and hoped that a regional collective security pact could put the West in a stronger diplomatic and military position for negotiations. On March 29, 1954, Secretary Dulles announced the American intention to pursue such a policy: "Under the conditions of today, the imposition on Southeast Asia of the political system of Communist Russia and its Chinese Communist ally, by whatever means, would be a grave threat to the whole free community. The United States feels that possibility should not be passively accepted but should be met by united action."[2]

In Congress, the only party leader to make any comments on Dulles' speech was Senator Knowland who called it "excellent" and stated: "It spelled out the policy of this government in Southeast Asia." Yet, in describing its implications, Knowland indicated the vagueness of the policy. "In some cases, it might mean action through the United Nations; and some through New Zealand, and in some through South Korea and Nationalist China."[3]

In early April, Congress' feelings on united action were revealed in a high level conference between leading administration and congressional figures. When the administration raised the idea of American intervention in Indochina, strong objections were expressed to any unilateral American intervention. Senator Lyndon Johnson asked if Dulles had consulted nations who might be possible allies in this endeavor and why the United Nations was not used as in the Korean case. To these questions, the secretary replied the United States had not consulted either with other nations or international bodies. This evident opposition by congressional leaders to unilateral intervention spurred Dulles to implement his previously announced threat of united action, and to begin determined efforts to organize SEATO.

At a meeting in the White House between key administration officials on the following night, the ramifications of the April 3 meeting became clear. In his memoirs, Eisenhower wrote that Dulles had concluded it

IV. The Creation of the Southeast Asia Treaty Organization

would be possible to get congressional authorization for American intervention only as part of a coalition, including the other free nations of Southeast Asia, the Philippines, and the British Commonwealth as well as a continued military effort by the French. Eisenhower stated: "There was nothing in these preconditions or in this congressional viewpoint with which I could disagree; my judgment entirely coincided with theirs."[4] Since both the executive and the Congress favored a multinational approach, some sort of Southeast Asian alliance seemingly would have to be created before the United States could intervene in Indochina.

On the same day, Eisenhower wrote to Prime Minister Winston Churchill urging cooperation in the formation of a regional security organization. In describing the nature and purpose of this alliance, he wrote: "I have in mind, in addition to our two countries, France, the Associated States, Australia, New Zealand, Thailand, and the Philippines. The United States government would expect to play its full part in such a coalition.... The important thing is that the coalition must be strong and it must be willing to join the fight, if necessary. I do not envisage the need of any appreciable ground forces on your or our part."[5]

United States policy, after the early April meeting, involved creating a regional defense organization for Southeast Asia that would be capable of preventing further Communist gains. The agreement of the prospective participants, it was hoped, would be obtained before the Geneva conference opened, primarily to strengthen the negotiating position of France and thus permit the French to resist Communist demands. Secondly, it entailed creating the appearance or possibility of American intervention. This would deter Chinese and Soviet intervention in the war, and would persuade the Russians that they must press the Chinese and the Vietminh to make concessions to the French. Thirdly, in the event the Geneva conference failed to achieve peace in Indochina and the war continued, the United States would continue to supply credits and equipment to the French. If it appeared that the Communists were undeterred by American threats and the new defense organization, collective intervention could be undertaken to prevent the loss of all of Southeast Asia to the Communists.

During the first week in April, administration officials contacted the ambassadors of New Zealand, Australia, the Philippines, Thailand, South Korea, and Taiwan in an attempt to secure their assent to such a coalition. In addition, the joint issuance by the allies of a warning to China against intervening in Indochina was also discussed.

Bystanders to the Vietnam War

Almost immediately, the administration's efforts met a rebuff from the two principal non–American members of the prospective coalition. The French refused to cooperate, explaining that French public opinion would not understand why the government had not done more to find a peaceful solution. Also, the united front tactic might harden the attitude of the Chinese and produce unfavorable conditions for negotiations at Geneva; it might even serve as a pretext for Chinese intervention. The British, who were equally reluctant, preferred not to take any steps that might jeopardize the chance of success at Geneva.

Throughout the remainder of April, Dulles tried to line up the free world allies to create at least a credible threat of intervention should the peace conference fail. He was supported in this effort by a number of Senate leaders, particularly Republicans. On April 8, several key Republican senators warned the allies that future foreign aid might depend on their willingness to join the United States in a common front during the current crisis. Senator Knowland was one of the leaders of this group. Referring to British and French reluctance to back united action, he declared: "Since some of the nations with which we are associated have been suggesting that they wait until after the Geneva conference before deciding how to respond to Secretary Dulles' inquiries regarding a collective action that would follow further aggression in Southeast Asia, I find there is a growing sentiment in Congress that perhaps Congress should delay until Geneva before setting any final policy in appropriations in support of NATO countries."[6]

Thus assured of a substantial degree of support in the Senate, Dulles left on April 10 to try to bring England and France in line with his policy of united action. In London, Dulles felt that he had won agreement to begin at once to create this united front in Southeast Asia with the idea that this would lead to united action, if necessary, to save Indochina. An Anglo-American communiqué said that the two nations were ready to take part in examining the possibilities of a Southeast Asia defense pact. Dulles, who believed the drafting of the pact could begin immediately, then flew to Paris where he discussed the proposed pact with French leaders. A Franco-American communiqué followed closely the language of the one issued in London.

The apparent "agreement" by Britain and France, however, did not reflect their actual positions. In the case of Britain, there was a case of genuine misunderstanding, with Dulles reading too much into the agree-

IV. The Creation of the Southeast Asia Treaty Organization

ment. France, in a desperate military situation, was also unable to make any commitment; she was torn between powerful "peace at any price" forces at home and a desire for greater Western aid.

One week later, the British temporarily halted momentum toward the creation of SEATO when their ambassador in Washington was specifically ordered not to attend a SEATO planning session. Dulles felt the British had switched their position because of objections from Prime Minister Nehru of India. British foreign Secretary Anthony later wrote in his memoirs that his objection was to the timing of the proposal: to proclaim SEATO before the Geneva Conference "would be unlikely to help us militarily and would harm us politically, by frightening off important potential allies."[7]

In mid–April, Senator Knowland again injected himself in this controversy in another attempt to revitalize the project. Knowland, fearful of communism as a "global menace," was a firm believer in a military alliance of the Philippines, Thailand, Cambodia, Laos, Vietnam, and the republics of China and Korea as the answer to the Communist threat in Indochina. On April 17, he reacted vigorously to Vice President Nixon's speech suggesting the possibility of unilateral American intervention in Vietnam. "Congress and the people," he said, "would not be satisfied with having this country assume 90% of the burden as it did in Korea." Knowland believed that United States ground forces would not be required in any event. "There is ample manpower among the free nations of Asia to meet the threat in Southeast Asia if supported by the air and sea forces of other nations with the potential to do so."[8]

Three days later, Senator Knowland clarified his views on SEATO, and fitted them into his belief that no American troops should be sent to Indochina. In a meeting of several congressional leaders and Secretary Dulles, Knowland urged the administration to include South Korea and Nationalist China in the proposed alliance. Presumably, these nations would supply the necessary manpower for any military action which might be necessary in Indochina.

That same day, Knowland's view received support from Senator William Jenner who severely attacked the administration's proposed alignment of nations for SEATO. "Filipinos and other Asian nations may wish to join in holding the line against the Red forces. That is their business. But Americans do not want any Pacific NATO, made up of weak sisters. We do not want any Pacific Treaty Organization made up mostly of

European colonial powers. Jenner concluded by advocating rather drastic remedies to the Asian Communist problem; he urged that the United States arm South Korea and Nationalist China so they could curb the Red Chinese menace once and for all."[9]

Yet opposition by Britain helped defeat Knowland's and Jenner's plans, and by the end of April, there would clearly be no SEATO in the immediate future to intervene in Indochina. The American delegation to the Geneva Conference, where the United States was attempting to organize the alliance, conceded that several months would be required to negotiate the pact. Secretary Dulles explained to Knowland that he had to start with nations, including Britain, that were unwilling to associate with Nationalist China. Britain's unwillingness to act at all was declared on April 27 by Churchill's announcement to Parliament that "we have not entered into any new political or military commitments"[10]

At this time, the purpose of SEATO was altered. On May 5, Dulles reported to congressional leaders that the United States had virtually abandoned all hope of effective united action in Vietnam and that he was now seeking a collective security system designed to seal off and protect Laos and Cambodia.

In early May, Senator Knowland attempted to resolve this dilemma by recommending the United States act without the cooperation of Britain. He suggested that President Eisenhower proceed without waiting for the outcome at Geneva, and if necessary, without British support, to draw up an allied defensive front in the Pacific. Senator Alexander Smith concurred, stating that while it was "a great blow that our British friends felt they must object to united action at this time," it was nevertheless imperative for the United States to go forward quickly with the pact concept.[11] The *New York Times* reported, however, that other powerful Republicans and Democrats opposed suggestions that the United States should attempt to act in Asia without Britain.[12]

The problems encountered in creating SEATO led to its becoming a partisan issue in the Senate by early May. Dulles's problems in organizing the united front at Geneva opened the first all-out Democratic attack on the Eisenhower administration's foreign policy. Declaring that the administration was alienating our allies, Senator Lyndon Johnson said that the administration had put the United States "in clear danger of being naked and alone in a hostile world." Senator Estes Kefauver claimed that previous partisan denunciation of Democratic foreign policy by the Republicans had made it

IV. The Creation of the Southeast Asia Treaty Organization

"doubtful whether in our time, in cases of limited aggression, that the forces of the nations of the free world can again be united in active opposition to it." Senator Wayne Morse charged Secretary Dulles with a series of "tragic blunders" that had alienated this country's allies and lost us Nehru of India.[13]

Put on the defensive, the Republicans tended to unite more closely. When President Eisenhower declared that progress was being made on the alliance, the *New York Times* reported a warmer Republican congressional attitude toward Dulles and a tendency of the Republicans to draw together. In part, this added support for Dulles also reflected the longtime support of a Pacific pact by Congress, especially since the rise of talk that American intervention might become necessary.

Despite Eisenhower's declaration of progress being made, vital differences with the British remained, especially regarding the scope of the proposed alliance. The British, increasingly alarmed about the threat to Malaya, were prepared to join with the United States, Australia, New Zealand and several Asiatic powers in some kind of a limited security pact for Indochina and the rest of Southeast Asia.

By now, Dulles had come to realize that he could not get united action with the British, French, the Australians, and the New Zealanders for anything but a very limited military operation in Indochina. James Reston of the *New York Times* noted: "they may unite to deny the conquest of the whole peninsula to the Communists, but they would not aim at total victory in Indochina any more than they did in Korea."[14]

Throughout the month of May, Dulles attempted to reconcile these differing objectives and viewpoints. By mid–May, Dulles bowed to British pressure by announcing the United States, while pressing for an alliance to save all of Southeast Asia, would save at least the essential parts if that were the only recourse. Dulles envisaged the inclusion of all the Associated States, but he added the United States would continue the effort to create such an alliance even if all or part of Indochina should be lost.

One of the major problems still to be reconciled was the composition of the alliance. A consequence of the allied divisions was a renewal by Washington of the suggestion that Britain be bypassed. Following upon Knowland's earlier suggestion, President Eisenhower told his press conference on May 19 that it might be possible to create a collective security system in Southeast Asia without the British, and that the United States might possibly work out something with Australia, New Zealand, and some Asian nations.

Bystanders to the Vietnam War

Yet almost immediately, this idea was dashed. On the following day, New Zealand's External Affairs Minister commented, "I can't conceive of a satisfactory alliance being made that would not include Britain," and said he felt "that any form of security pact for Southeast Asia will in fact include Britain."[15] Historian Charles Lerche claimed that the United States took this bold, seemingly tactless, diplomatic step, and several others during this time, in an attempt to "shock" Britain into acting on SEATO.[16]

With the question of British participation apparently settled, Senator Mansfield revealed other reservations concerning the membership of the proposed alliance. The senator noted with dismay the European predominance of the future SEATO. "I think that we ought to place priority not on the creation of a Southeast Asia pact manned entirely by white nations.... I think rather than that, what we ought to have is a Southeast Asia pact based primarily on Asiatic nations in that area.... And I would like to see laid down in that area a sort of a Monroe Doctrine, perhaps by Nehru, which would be somewhat comparable to the Monroe Doctrine issued by our own country, with the idea in mind that behind this Asiatic pact would be the might of the United States and other interested nations."[17] These views by Mansfield closely corresponded to those being set down by the British.

Commenting at the same time, Knowland took a somewhat different viewpoint. He agreed on broader Asian representation, but disagreed on holding up the pact until India was willing to join. The attempt to broaden Asian participation had foundered when India, Indonesia, and Burma refused to join. He also reiterated his earlier belief that Formosa and South Korea be included in the pact. Like Mansfield, he stressed the use of Asiatic ground forces should the need to deploy combat troops develop; both men opposed a reliance on American ground troops in Southeast Asia.

Throughout the remainder of May, the SEATO question seemed deadlocked when on June 23, British foreign secretary Anthony Eden suggested a dual approach to the problem. First, he advocated banning aggression by reciprocal arrangement that involved both the Communist bloc and the free nations of the East and the West, along the line of the 1925 Treaty of Locarno. The main purpose of the proposal for a Far Eastern "Locarno" was to join the Colombo powers—India, Pakistan, Ceylon, Burma, and Indonesia—with the Western powers in a joint guarantee of whatever Far Eastern settlement may be reached. His second suggestion

IV. The Creation of the Southeast Asia Treaty Organization

involved a defensive alliance similar to the North Atlantic Treaty Organization.

The Locarno Pact was a 1925 agreement among seven European countries to guarantee the border between Germany, France, and Belgium after World War I. It dealt with the Rhineland, a German-speaking area lying between the three nations which was then occupied by France. The agreement was to be enforced by England and Italy who pledged to resist whatever country challenged this arrangement. When Germany violated the Pact in 1936 by occupying this disputed area, no action was taken. The Locarno idea, being revived by the British, became a famous symbol of diplomatic failure on the road to World War II.

The British suggestions were dealt with in late June during the visit of Churchill and Eden to Washington. In the jointly issued "Potomac Charter," the United States and Britain agreed to move forward at once to form plans for the defense of Southeast Asia. However, they agreed in effect not to put any of the plans into action until France's new premier had an opportunity to make peace with the Communists; he had established his own deadline of July 20 for reaching an armistice. The Anglo-American communiqué, however, did not mention the British proposal that the Southeast Asia defense pact be accompanied by a "Locarno-type" compact of reciprocal nonaggression pledges between the pro–Western and Communist powers.

The administration was obviously under pressure from the Senate not to concede too much to the British. For example, Senator Pat McCarren, in a speech shortly after the end of the Eisenhower-Churchill talks, accused the administration of "subverting its own judgment" in foreign policy to that of Britain whose position he sharply attacked.

In the next few days, the United States openly announced its opposition to the "Locarno" idea. On June 30, Eisenhower declared the United States would not enter into any nonaggression pact in Southeast Asia that might oblige it to fight against any peoples that make war to gain their freedom from Communist domination. The president said: "I will not be a party to any agreements that makes anybody a slave."[18] There was substantial political backing for Eisenhower's decision. Both the Republicans and Democrats were almost unanimous in their support of suggestions by Dulles for an effective Southeast Asia pact and in opposition to the British proposal for a mutual defense arrangement that included the Communists.

Bystanders to the Vietnam War

Throughout July and August, there remained several serious differences between Britain and the United States over SEATO. One concerned the membership of the proposed alliance; Great Britain insisted upon the widest possible representation of Asian states, whereas the United States was satisfied with a treaty whose only Asian adherents were Thailand and the Philippines. More fundamental was the disagreement over the nature of the pact. The United States was thinking in terms of a military alliance of the NATO-ANZUS type; the British were pressing a program which would deal more with the "complex, economic, social, and cultural problems of the area."

By mid–August, a compromise over these issues was reached. The type of pact agreed upon was neither the tightly-knit arrangements with the unified military command, as proposed by the United States, nor the loose confederation bound together only by common economic interests that the British had urged. Instead, it was decided that the new treaty would require each party to make a firm commitment to the defense of Southeast Asia without spelling out the nature or extent of the guarantee afforded. It did not contain an automatic military obligation, nor a Marshall Plan–type financial provision. The member nations bound themselves only to "meet common dangers" in accordance with their own "constitutional processes" and to "consult" with each other.

The members of SEATO were the United States, Great Britain, France, Australia, New Zealand, Thailand, the Philippines, and Pakistan. The SEATO alliance had great significance for Indochina. Although forbidden to join an alliance under the Geneva Accords, South Vietnam, Laos, and Cambodia were to be protected by a separate protocol. According to the alliance, a threat to them would endanger the peace and security of the members. Dulles hoped that the mere existence of the alliance might deter Communist aggression.

Considering its membership, SEATO was basically a Western alliance, rather than Asian. It had no standing army and did not adopt the "all for one" principle, as contained in NATO. SEATO's opposition to Communist aggression appeared to be more theoretical than actual,

In the hearings before the Foreign Relations Committee, the Senate showed its keen interest over the implications of this treaty which it had advocated throughout the Indochina crisis. Because the administration was particularly concerned that the session of Congress should not close without some preliminary consideration being given to the treaty, the

IV. The Creation of the Southeast Asia Treaty Organization

committee decided to act with unusual dispatch. Accordingly, the first public hearing was held on November 11, 1954, the morning after the president had transmitted the pertinent documents to the Senate. It was hoped that such a demonstration of continued interest in the pact would provide additional impetus to other signatories to proceed promptly with their own ratification.

One of the main issues to arise in the hearings in January 1955 was the possible involvement of the United States in war through obligations contained in the pending treaty. Because the administration showed a deep concern over Congress' war-making initiative, the SEATO treaty incorporated a process deemed by Secretary Dulles as the Monroe Doctrine formula. This meant that each nation, not automatically compelled to act, would act according to its own interests as the United States historically had done via the Monroe Doctrine in the Western Hemisphere. Specifically, Article IV of the treaty read as follows: "Each party recognizes that aggression by means of any attack in the treaty area against any of the parties or against any state or territory which the parties by unanimous agreement may hereafter designate, would endanger its own peace and safety, and agrees that it will in that event act to meet the common danger in accordance with its constitutional process."

This article, as defined by Dulles, meant that the president would consult with Congress in case of any threat of danger "unless the emergency were so great that prompt action was necessary to save the vital interests of the United States." Otherwise, "the normal process would be to act through Congress, if it were in session, and if not in session, to call Congress."[19] Recalling the heated debate in the Senate over this issue during the hearings on NATO, and doubtless bearing in mind Congress' recent great reluctance to go to war over Indochina, Dulles wished to avoid a repetition of this rancor on the pending treaty. He stated at the hearings: "The practical difference between the two approaches—NATO and the Monroe Doctrine—from the standpoint of giving security to the other parties was not appreciable, and it was better to avoid a formula which would reopen the constitutional debate as to the relative powers of the president and the Congress under these different formulas."[20]

During the January hearings, the question of the war-making power was again vigorously discussed. One of the witnesses suggested the need of an amendment to the treaty which would read: "No United States ground, air or naval forces shall engage in any defense actions in accordance with the provisions of this treaty before the Congress has consented to their use against Communist armed attack or armed aggression by a declaration of war."[21] This proposal led to a searching discussion in executive session. It was finally rejected as throwing open the entire controversial topic of the relative powers of the executive and legislative branches. The committee was content with assurances by Dulles that Eisenhower would not ignore Congress' prerogatives. In its report, however, the committee declared: "The treaty in no way affects the basic division of authority between the president and the Congress as defined in the Constitution. In no way does it alter the constitutional relationship between them. In particular, it does not increase, decrease, or change the power of the president as commander-in-chief of the armed forces or impair the full authority of Congress to declare war."[22]

This debate over the constitutional war-making powers had great significance in view of the instability of the Southeast Asia area, much of which took the form of possible revolutionary insurrection rather than overt aggression. Consequently, the committee took great care to clarify the United States' obligations should insurrection occur. Senator Alexander Smith queried Dulles: "If there is subversive activity which is threatening the integrity of South Vietnam, would we feel that we were called upon under the treaty to give a danger signal and get together with our allies and consider it?"[23] Dulles answered directly: "If that situation arises or threatens, we should consult together immediately in order to agree on measures which should be taken. That is an obligation for consultation. It is not an obligation for action."[24]

The obligations undertaken by the United States under the SEATO treaty were consistent with the feelings of both Great Britain and the Senate. Both were very reluctant to engage the West in ground combat against the Communist forces in Indochina. For the Senate, this treaty provided at least a psychological vent against the Communists, while reflecting its reluctance to actually commit itself to combat. Although the Senate played a relatively minor direct role in the creation of SEATO, its sentiments were respected by the limited responsibility entailed by the treaty.

Political scientist Hans Morganthau wrote that SEATO was merely a psychological gesture by the United States government. He noted:

> It can be stated on excellent authority that when SEATO was conceived in the fall of 1954, it was intended not as a measure of military policy, but of psychological warfare. It was intended to counteract the psychological damage which the parti-

IV. The Creation of the Southeast Asia Treaty Organization

tion of Vietnam at the Geneva Conference of 1954 had inflicted upon the prestige of the West, the United States included. It was intended as a gesture of defiance, as an act which would convey the appearance of initiative and strength where actual initiative and strength were lacking. As such, SEATO was slated to take its place in that series of portentous, yet hollow pronouncements which ranged from the "unleashing of Chiang Kai-shek" through "agonizing reappraisal" and the "New Look" defense policy.[25]

While SEATO may have been a "psychological gesture" to some extent at the time of its inception, this was not true ten years later. It would then be used as the legal justification for American intervention in Vietnam.

V

The Geneva Conference

The Geneva Conference, lasting from April to July 1954, was the subject of much controversy in the United States, even before it actually took place. The Senate brought heavy political pressure against its meeting, and later this pressure served to guide the administration in its dealings at Geneva. At the end of the conference, when a settlement for Indochina had been reached, the Senate's opposition encouraged the Eisenhower administration to refrain from signing the final agreements.

The Geneva Conference was agreed upon by the big four powers (the United States, Britain, France, and Russia) at a foreign ministers conference held in Berlin in February 1954 to discuss Asian problems. Previously the United States had been opposed to such a conference because Communist China would surely be invited. But the French government, under pressure from the peace movement in France, threatened to abstain from the proposed European Defense Community and forced the United States to reverse its former opposition.

France was especially anxious for the conference to meet. She was hopeful that the new Navarre military strategy for Vietnam would lead to a great victory for her, and enable France to obtain a victor's peace at the conference. Ironically, the fortress at Dien Bien Phu surrendered on the day that the conference began, seriously compromising the Western position.

When Secretary Dulles returned from Berlin, there was much senatorial criticism to his assent to the forthcoming Indochina conference (a decision made without consulting congressional leaders). Primarily, this opposition centered around fears of possible recognition of Communist China and strong anxiety, lest there be a "Far Eastern Munich" (a reference to the 1938 betrayal of Czechoslovakia to Nazi Germany by England and France). Dulles attempted to deal with the former objection by insisting

V. The Geneva Conference

upon, and obtaining at the last hour of the Berlin conference, an agreement that the Geneva meeting did not any way imply recognition by the United States of the Peking regime. But to several senators, notably Homer Ferguson, William Knowland, Styles Bridges, and Alexander Smith, such a written notice was not enough. Senator Ferguson, chairman of the Senate Republican policy committee and normally a supporter of administration foreign policy, declared: "Russia for a long time has been trying to obtain recognition for Communist China in the family of nations."[1] He also feared the meeting would have great propaganda value for Russia and the Communists generally.

Secretary Dulles, in a series of meetings with influential Republican and Democratic senators in late February, attempted to ease the Senate's reservations about the conference. He explained there was no way to avoid a meeting with Communist China on Indochina without facing serious consequences in France. The United States had already negotiated a previous truce, dealing with Korea, with the Chinese Communists. Also, Foreign Minister George Bidault had insisted that French public opinion would not understand the United States policy of refusing either to fight or to negotiate with Communist China on Indochina. Such a policy, he was told, would probably strengthen the neutralists in France who claimed the United States was willing to fight to the last Frenchman, and it almost certainly would prove disastrous to getting the French National Assembly's approval for the European Defense Community. This meant that France might refuse to commit troops to the NATO alliance, one of the United States' main tools for protecting Western Europe.

Despite these arguments, Congress remained very cool to the proposed conference. The majority of the Republicans indicated to Dulles that the administration alone would be held responsible for the outcome at Geneva and that the congressional wing of the party would hold him accountable for any "slip" there. "Slip" was defined to mean, first, any suggestion that the United States was moving toward any form of recognition of Communist China and, second, any action that might involve the United States in a war in Indochina. The *New York Times* reported that a private inquiry among highly placed Republicans in both the Senate and the House made it plain that the Republicans would give to the Geneva discussions what Senator Knowland called "close scrutiny"; that if the Geneva talks turned out not to their satisfaction, Dulles could expect a general attack from all save the most advanced internationalists in the Republican

Party.² At this time, the Democrats generally adopted an attitude of "severe aloofness" from the whole affair; their criticisms would come later when the Geneva Conference became a partisan issue.

Senator Knowland, spokesman for the congressional Republican bloc insisting on a "hard" policy toward Asian communism, was one of the most severe critics. On February 22, he delivered a speech, sharply critical of Dulles's action in agreeing to the Geneva meeting. Knowland could find no justification for the United States consent to inclusion of the Indochina problem on the Geneva calendar. The coming Asia conference in Geneva must not become a "Far Eastern Munich" that would lead to the admission of Communist China into the United Nations. He also stated (just two and a half months before the fall of Dien Bien Phu) that "communism now hopes to gain at the conference table what it did not gain on the battlefield."³

On February 24, testifying before the Senate Foreign Relations Committee, Dulles showed some resentment against criticism of the agreements to bring Communist China into the Geneva Conference. When Senator Smith asked him whether he thought the invitation to Communist China gave too much recognition to the Peking regime, Dulles replied that he had won every point in his dispute with the Russians on the Geneva Conference. Dulles recalled that the United States had been trying for months to get Communist China into a conference on the future of Korea, and one which would also include the Soviet Union.

In the last month before the conference convened, the Senate's pressure against appeasement fitted in with the administration's "hard" policy. Late in March, Assistant Secretary of State for Far Eastern Affairs Walter Robertson announced that the United States would make no "dangerous or fatal concessions" at Geneva. On March 29, Secretary Dulles made a very significant address in which he urged united action to deal with the Communist threat in Indochina. The secretary hoped to strengthen the West's bargaining position at Geneva by creating an alliance strong enough to intervene should the Communists prove overbearing in the negotiations. By uniting allied strength, the deteriorating French position could be shored up in the upcoming talks. Dulles's speech also warned the Communists not to push the West too far or else face the risk of Western intervention in the war.

Having expressed its initial reservations about the Geneva Conference, the Senate muted its criticism and attempted to help Dulles secure

V. The Geneva Conference

allied unity at Geneva. On April 8, Senate Republican leaders warned the allies that future foreign aid might depend on their willingness to join the United States in a common front in the Indochina crisis. In more conciliatory terms, Senator Mansfield publicly stressed the need for greater allied and domestic unity before the conference convened.

At this time, a political equilibrium appeared to have been created with both parties rallying around the administration. The Democrats, though generally still dissatisfied by the lack of clarity over ultimate administration purposes in Indochina, took the position that Dulles had to be supported wholeheartedly for the present. The Republicans, though also ready to back Dulles for the time being, looked toward Geneva with "foreboding." The *New York Times* reported, "No secretary of state in recent memory undertook a foreign mission with a colder background of congressional nonsupport than that which will chill John Foster Dulles as he sets off for Geneva. For the conference there is regarded by the majority of the Republicans in Congress as an enormous threat. In the Senate, it is universally so regarded by those Republicans who are most powerful on the domestic scene."[4]

By early May, the administration was adopting a more moderate position toward a settlement of the Southeast Asia problem; this change reflected the increasing likelihood that there would be no impending allied or United States intervention. French public opinion was moving toward a "peace at any price" attitude, and Great Britain was reluctant to act militarily until the Geneva Conference was given a chance to make peace in Indochina. The United States had hoped that the threat of intervention alone would be sufficient to make the Communists draw back, but instead this threat produced so much opposition in Congress and in Britain that it lost most of its effectiveness. Furthermore, the administration was hindered by domestic political considerations and by its taking such a tough propaganda line against the Communists. Senator Joseph Tydings analyzed Dulles's dilemma, stating that the secretary "was forbidden by dominant elements in Congress, and by his own comments, to deal with Communist China or Ho Chi Minh. Thus he cannot negotiate with or fight against the Vietminh and their Communist Chinese allies."[5]

The administration's more moderate position entailed a greater stress on compromise to reach a negotiated settlement. The Senate was not long in responding to this apparent change in policy. Dulles' action in publicizing united action on the eve of the Geneva Conference, and then being rebuffed by the allies, came under criticism. Senator Knowland proposed that the United States immediately draw a line against further Communist aggression in Asia. He stated clearly that he had written off the Geneva Conference and was resentful of Britain's refusal to consider taking action until the Geneva discussions had ended. Knowland was afraid that an "Asian Munich" might occur at Geneva, and that the administration was not making an urgent effort to create an allied front in Asia.

During a bipartisan congressional hearing on May 5, Dulles defended his policies, at a time when these policies were becoming caught up in partisan politics. The Republican Party tended to support the secretary in fear that the Geneva results might ultimately become for the Democrats, a rallying cry much as the "appeasement" of Chinese communism had been charged to the Democrats by the Republicans. The Democrats maintained for the time being the silence that had characterized their attitude since before the Geneva Conference opened.

The following day, Dulles had rather optimistic comments regarding a settlement at Geneva. The United States, Britain, and France substantially agreed on a compromise plan for a "protected armistice" in Indochina which entailed an independent Laos and Cambodia and a partitioned Vietnam. Dulles told a number of congressional leaders that if France and the Associated States held firm, it might be possible to get the major allies to agree to a political guarantee of the "protected armistice" and a sort of multilateral "Monroe Doctrine" for the whole of Southeast Asia.

Despite Dulles' hopeful comments, the Democrats launched at this time a strong partisan attack on the administration's Indochina policy. The most serious charges were levied by Senator Lyndon Johnson who stated the results thus far of the Geneva Conference make it "apparent that American foreign policy has never in all its history suffered such a stunning reversal. We have been caught bluffing by our enemies. Our friends and allies are frightened and wondering where we are headed."[6] Senator Guy Gillette accused the administration of falling into "a diplomatic disaster" in Geneva, leading to "the collapse of American leadership among the free nations." Senator Theodore Greene asserted that the nation was being "isolated from its friends about as fast as the administration can grind out new policy statements. The allies fear we are inviting war."

On May 7, shortly after the Democratic attacks, the administration shored up its moderate stands. Reporting on the Geneva Conference, Sec-

V. The Geneva Conference

retary Dulles told the nation that the United States would be "gravely concerned" if the outcome at Geneva should "provide a road to a Communist takeover of the region and further aggression. If this occurs, or if hostilities continue, then the need will be even more urgent to create the conditions for united action in defense of the area."[7]

Within a few days, there were additional strong Democratic criticisms of the administration's Indochina policy, despite Dulles's stern warning to the Communists. Senator Estes Kefauver asserted that United States leadership of the free world was at its "lowest point" since the beginning of World War II. The Geneva Conference had been a "failure" largely because the Senate had sent Dulles there "with his hands tied behind his back." United States leaders, he said, had been "misinformed and confused" about the situation in Indochina and had "vacillated when they should have been firm." Senator George Smathers accused Britain and France of refusing to support this country at the conference, and he called for a reversal of the entire foreign aid program to make Latin America, rather than Europe, the main beneficiary.[8]

Senators Alexander Wiley and Alexander Smith, the senior Republican foreign policy spokesman in the Senate, came to the defense of the administration and sought to calm the scene. Senator Wiley appealed to the Senate to resist "the frustrations and irritations of the moment." Smith asserted that President Eisenhower and Secretary Dulles were entitled to "the highest possible tributes for the real accomplishments they have achieved in the face of the greatest of odds."[9]

By the end of May, the administration had decided on its general policy at Geneva. Partition would be the best possible deal for the French. Any attempt by the Communists to take over the entire Indochina peninsula would probably force the United States into the war. The *New York Times* reported a widespread sentiment that the split in Washington, like the split in the coalition, would end if the only alternative to a compromise armistice was unconditional surrender. It further reported a general agreement in Washington that Congress would back the president on a fight or surrender proposition.[10]

On June 11, Dulles stressed this theme that the United States would not acquiesce in a policy of "peace at any price." While the government and people of the United States want peace, he said, they do not propose to buy it the price of surrender. The simultaneous presentation of both peace and vital national interests required support of the government "by a people who are willing, if need be, to sacrifice to preserve the vital interests."[11]

Despite these determined remarks, the Western position seem to be in sharp disarray by mid–June. A steady deterioration in the French military position and an impending government crisis seemed likely to bring a "peace at any price" cabinet into office. There was a growing conviction among Western diplomats that the only terms the Communist representatives at Geneva would accept would be tantamount to surrender by France and the Associated States.

These ominous developments evoked strong criticism in the Senate from both sides of the aisle. Senator Knowland demanded an end to the Geneva conference and suggested that Vietnam, Laos, and Cambodia might declare their independence, and appeal to the United Nations for help, if France accepted "peace at any price." Speaking in equally critical terms, Senator Hubert Humphrey stated: "We had our bluff called two or three times in the last month. We have been defeated at Geneva.... I believe we went to Geneva without being in a position of strength. Our representatives went to Geneva after the budget had been cut, and there had been put into effect a reduction in the Air Force. The Soviet Union made us look sick at Geneva. The Chinese Communists, as well as the Soviet Communists, have gained a great victory there."[12]

Senator Hubert Humphrey, who urged support for South Vietnam during the 1950s (U.S. Senate Historical Office).

In the second half of June, Indochina diplomacy approached a climax. The "peace" government of Pierre Mendes-France took office on June 18. It was soon apparent that he was prepared to cede to the Communists large areas of Indochina in return for a settlement. On June 28, the United States and Britain agreed to let the French government take the initiative in negotiating with the Communists at Geneva. But at the same time,

V. *The Geneva Conference*

the two governments warned the Communist powers that "the international situation will be seriously aggravated" if the French were "confronted with demands which prevent an acceptable agreement regarding Indochina." Eisenhower stated he would not enter into any agreements that subordinated people to foreign domination against their will. The joint communiqué signified that the United States would not fight to prevent the partition of Indochina, and it would agree not to upset the settlements. During these Anglo-American talks, Churchill also stated that eventually Communist China would have to be taken into the United Nations, a policy strongly opposed by the United States.

The policy of the Mendes-France government and the moderate compromise which resulted from the Anglo-American talks led to widespread congressional hostilities to the Indochina negotiations. Senator Knowland intimated that the Geneva negotiations were the first step in "a major effort to bring Communist China into the United Nations." He put forward a legislative rider for United States withdrawal from the United Nations if Communist China were accepted.

Knowland was unalterably opposed to the admission of Communist China into the United Nations. He stated on July 1, 1954: "On the day that Communist China is voted into membership into the United Nations, I shall resign my majority leadership in the Senate so that without embarrassment to any of my colleagues or to the administration, I can devote my full efforts in the Senate and throughout the country to terminate United States membership in that organization and our financial support to it."[13]

Of the many powerful senators from both parties who supported the Knowland position, Senator Pat McCarron was among the most vitriolic in his criticism. He declared in the Senate on June 28, "We must stop kidding ourselves about the results of the Geneva Conference. There can be no question whatever about the fact that the net effect of the Geneva Conference has been a serious blow to the prestige of the United States, a serious loss of face by the Western world throughout Asia, and a tremendous victory for Mao Tse-tung and his servant, Chou En-lai, and for the cause of communism throughout Asia. No one unsympathetic with communism has gained anything of lasting value from this conference."[14]

As the Geneva Conference moved toward its climax in July, the Senate continued to fulminate against the administration. In a speech on July 8, Senator Mansfield criticized the executive for not taking the Senate into his confidence. He cited his own earlier Senate opposition to the United States participating at Geneva until Allied differences had been resolved. Participation under the current circumstances was an error, and "there is reason to believe that the terms are likely to be more unfavorable than they would otherwise have been, had this country steered clear of the entire business."[15] He noted the Senate had helped prevent the United States from militarily intervening, and felt that it should have been consulted on the Geneva Conference, too.

Mansfield also disapproved of the brazen tactics used throughout the Indochina crisis. "There has been too much 'bluff' in this administration, contrary to the period of the administration of Theodore Roosevelt, when the slogan was 'speak softly, but carry a big stick.' I think some of the officials of the administration are speaking loudly but carrying a feather duster, because they do not have anything with which to back up the statements they make. They talk about a 'New Look' [defense policy], when we have 50 ships in mothballs and a large reduction in the naval force."[16]

The next day, Senator Homer Ferguson rallied to the defense of the administration. In particular, he directed his remarks to Mansfield's suggestion that the collapse of the French position in Indochina was due to the United States' going along with the French demand that it should have a peace conference at Geneva prior to a unified position. "It is absurd to attribute French weakness, its loss of the will to fight, the loss of Dien Bien Phu, and so forth, to the Geneva Conference. The French were determined to talk of peace and would have done so whether or not we consented."[17]

The stinging criticisms clearly had their effect on the administration. In response to Knowland's comments, Dulles stated the United States would use every means at its disposal, including the veto, to bar Peking from the United Nations. With Geneva obviously linked to "appeasement," the secretary further declared that neither he nor his deputy, Undersecretary Walter Bedell Smith, would attend the concluding phase of the conference.

In mid–July, the administration reversed this latter decision and decided to return representatives to the talks. Dulles explained this reversal in the same terms which he had used to explain the administration's original decision to participate in the talks back in February. "If we had ignored the French pleas to send Undersecretary Smith to Geneva, we would've damaged our position in Europe. Such a refusal on our part

V. The Geneva Conference

would have hurt chances for ratification of the EDC [European Defense Community] and possibly weaken the structure of NATO. The French people might have felt that the United States let them down."[18]

Despite the compelling logic of this position, the administration was careful to consider the Senate's sentiments. The joint communiqué issued by Dulles, British Foreign Secretary Anthony Eden, and French Premier Mendes-France announcing the return of the United States to the talks seemed directed particularly at the Senate. "Mr. John Foster Dulles explained fully the limitations which that government desires to observe as not itself having a primary responsibility in the Indochina war. Mr. Mendes-France expressed the view, with which Mr. Anthony Eden associated himself, that it would nevertheless serve the interest of peace and freedom in the area, if the United States, without departing from the principles which Mr. Dulles expressed, were once again to be represented at Geneva at the ministerial level."[19] Two days later, Undersecretary Smith left for Geneva.

The United States return to the negotiations did not signify a greater willingness to make concessions to the Communists. On July 14, United States and Britain announced that they had reached agreement on allied goals for a settlement for Indochina and for a contingency plan should the Communists reject their proposed settlement. The plan called for the partition of Vietnam, French-occupied enclaves in North Vietnam, exchange of populations between the two halves, and withdrawal of the Vietminh from the proposed French-occupied areas. If the Communists coerced the French into an unacceptable surrender, the United States and Britain would then set a line in Southeast Asia and make it known that the Communist powers could not advance over it without risking World War III. Simultaneously, the Allies would hasten to create a Southeast Asia defense pact to enforce this threat.

At the same time, the administration acted to keep clear of appeasement charges by the Senate. Secretary Dulles indicated the United States would not commit itself to any truce document ceding territory to the Communists. Simultaneously, the United States pledged to defend the non–Communist areas should the Communists renew their aggression in Indochina. On July 19, two days before the end of the conference, Dulles officially stated that the United States would not sign an Indochinese peace settlement; he also said the United States would not do anything to upset a reasonable settlement.

Bystanders to the Vietnam War

The controversial Geneva Conference concluded on July 21. The principal provisions of the accords were: hostilities were to cease; a military line of demarcation (not a political boundary) was to be in effect at approximately the 17th parallel; Vietnam was specifically declared a unified nation, not to be partitioned; elections were to be held by July 1956 throughout Vietnam to establish a democratic government; foreign troops were to be withdrawn; the introduction of arms and troops to the Indochinese states was forbidden; and an international control commission consisting of India, Canada, and Poland was set up to supervise the execution of the armistice agreement.

However, the agreement did not resolve the major issue of the war—Ho Chi Minh's desire to rule all of Vietnam. A Canadian diplomat stated: "The Geneva agreement was a hasty bargain accepted by all parties as the only way to avoid a dangerous confrontation."[20]

There were several factors behind the moderate positions, which included a pullout from Laos and Cambodia, taken by the Communists at Geneva. Historian John R. Beal wrote this was due to the Chinese fear of American intervention; to Russia's drive to kill the EDC by acting conciliatory to the French; and to a change in tactics by Communist China, from naked aggression to political penetration, as the means of extending her influence in the Far East.[21]

A strikingly different analysis was offered by British foreign secretary Anthony Eden who stressed the impact of the hydrogen bomb as a moderating influence on the powers at Geneva. "I do not believe that we should have got through the Geneva Conference and avoided a major war without it," he declared. He also was more pragmatic about the settlement. "I thought it unrealistic to expect that a victor's terms could be imposed upon an undefeated enemy."[22]

The American and British governments offered different views of the conference. Shortly after the Geneva Conference concluded, President Eisenhower indicated that the United States was accepting the settlement in Indochina in the spirit of making the best of a bad bargain. He acknowledged that the settlement contained features "which we do not like," though declining to describe the armistice as "appeasement" or "surrender."

The United States was not totally displeased with the Geneva Accords. Laos, Cambodia, and South Vietnam had maintained non–Communist governments. The United States was given a two-year window to build up

V. The Geneva Conference

the non–Communist forces in South Vietnam. It was also glad the French were being ousted. The U.S.–French partnership had not been a successful one. Although it had received $2.6 billion in U.S. military aid between 1950 and 1954, France had not been a cooperative ally. With French colonialism gone, the United States was more confident it could find a viable non–Communist alternative to the Communists.

As had been feared, the settlement produced some domestic political backlash. In the U.S. Senate, there was much bitterness expressed. Senator Knowland asserted the settlement was "the greatest victory the Communists have won in twenty years." Senators Stuart Symington and Edwin Johnson saw "appeasement."[23] Generally, Congress responded to the agreement with a mood of deep gloom and uncertainty.

On July 21, Senator Symington vigorously protested against the agreement at Geneva, which was indicative of the strong pressure on the Eisenhower administration at that time. He was distressed that "our recent policies in the Far East have been conducted over the direct protest of members of the Joint Chiefs of Staff. He believed there were members of the Joint Chiefs who agreed with many members of the Senate on both sides that the time for appeasement was over, and that the United States must make a stand somewhere, on some basis. He added that he was "very proud of those members Joint Chiefs of Staff who feel as they do in that connection."[24]

The *New York Times* reported that the Vietminh also were disappointed in the peace settlement, and expressed bitter feelings toward Russia and China. Members of the Vietminh delegation declared openly that pressure from Chinese foreign minister Chou En-lai and Russian foreign minister Vyachev Molotov forced their regime to accept less than it rightfully should have obtained.

Several senators were far more positive toward the settlement than had been the Eisenhower administration. Senator Kennedy stated: "I don't know why the Communists ever agreed to the settlement. They were on their way there." Senator Wiley clearly identified the contradictory nature of the critics' Indochina position. He said the critics had obviously been playing both sides of the fence simultaneously. "They condemned the Indochina to settlement, but most of them would've been totally unwilling to commit American manpower for the defense of Indochina…. Many of the critics of the present armistice never offered a reasonable practical alternative, and many of those same critics will be fighting tooth and nail against the United States military commitments for the proposed Southeast Asia Pact."[25]

The Geneva agreement led to the United States becoming the dominant Western power in Vietnam, rather than France. The French defeat had been costly; they had spent over $5 billion in military expenditures and suffered approximately 150,000 casualties. While regretting the loss of North Vietnam to the Communists, the Eisenhower administration saw the agreement as a chance for the United States to build support in South Vietnam in time for the 1956 elections. The loss of territory to the Communists had been temporarily contained. The United States would now extend massive aid to South Vietnam to save it for the West.

VI

The Quiet Years

During the period following the Geneva Conference until the end of the Eisenhower administration, the United States gradually grew more involved in Vietnam. American policy came to rest upon the survival and "success" of the Ngo Dinh Diem regime. Diem, whose rise to power was facilitated by several key senatorial contacts, was able to maintain his position, in large measure, through these contacts and by virtue of the anti–Communist feeling of the times. During the mid–1950s, the major battleground of the Cold War shifted from Europe to the new nations of Asia and Africa. The United States was extremely anxious to halt the spread of Communism, especially in South Vietnam. Despite certain obvious shortcomings, Cold War tensions tended to solidify Diem's American support by 1960.

Ngo Dinh Diem was a rarity in Asia, a pro–American, anti–Communist leader. Born the son of government officials, Diem attended French Catholic schools and the School for Public Administration in Hanoi. After finishing at the top of his class, Diem was given a government position. A devout Catholic, he became a staunch anti–Communist before he became a nationalist. Under the French, he rose to the position of Minister of the Interior which was the highest position in the government.

He later resigned when the French refused to follow his advice for reforms. For the next few years, first under the French and later from the Japanese, he refused all offers to serve in government. After World War II, he continued to refuse government service offers, even when threatened with deportation.

"Discovered" in Tokyo in 1950 by a Michigan State University professor, Diem was brought to the United States where he came under the protection of Francis Cardinal Spellman of New York and Joseph P. Kennedy, father of Senator John F. Kennedy. Arrangements were made to acquaint

President Eisenhower welcoming South Vietnamese leader Ngo Dinh Diem to the United States in 1957 (U.S. Air Force).

Diem with such importance political figures as Supreme Court Justice William Douglas, and senators John F. Kennedy and Mike Mansfield. Efforts were also made to gain support from the editors of the *New York Herald Tribune*, the *New York Times*, and *Time* and *Life* magazines. While in the United States, Diem settled in a Catholic monastery in New Jersey. He lectured widely, appealing for an independent, non–Communist Vietnam.

Originally the U.S. government had doubts about Diem, claiming that he was "too rigid, too Catholic, too monkish."[1] An elitist who lacked charism, he did not connect with the masses, detested other people, and trusted only his family. Eventually a channel of support was created, which helped persuade the Eisenhower administration to accept Diem as the democratic "hope" in South Vietnam. Working in Diem's favor were his strong pro–Western and anti–Communist beliefs.

VI. The Quiet Years

Within a short time, the American friends of Vietnam was created; this became the organ of the Vietnam lobby in the United States. Associated with this organization were such luminaries as senators John Kennedy and Richard Neuberger, journalist Max Lerner, historian Arthur Schlesinger, Jr., representatives Emmanuel Celler and Edna Kelly, and socialist leader Norman Thomas. According to political analysts Robert Scheer and Warren Hinckle, the Vietnam lobby was the ultimate product of the school of liberal Cold War anti-communism. In a period dominated by Senator Joseph McCarthy's anti–Communist rantings, these liberals could not espouse any other policy for Vietnam.[2]

Senator Mansfield's role in persuading the Eisenhower administration to back Diem was more direct than that of the Vietnam lobby, whose activities were less publicized. Under U.S. pressure, the Vietnamese emperor Bao Dai had appointed Diem in June 1954 to become prime minister. When the Diem regime seemed in jeopardy in the fall of 1954, Mansfield took an unequivocal position in support of it. The Montana senator stressed that Diem was the best hope for a non–Communist Vietnam. In his 1954 report, he urged: "In the event that the Diem government falls, the United States should consider an immediate suspension of all aid to Vietnam and the French Union forces there." Prophetically the report added:

> If [there was] an overthrow of Diem, it would raise in my opinion, serious doubts about the salvageability of any of our present policy with respect to Vietnam. The visible alternatives to the Diem governments are not promising. They are of the Vietminh absorption of the south or a government or succession of governments at Saigon in the pre–Diem pattern. Such governments made little effort to root themselves in the people in the past, and it is unlikely they will do so in the future. It is probable instead that they will continue to lean heavily and indefinitely on the prop of foreign support. Barring some drastic change in the total situation in Vietnam, such a government will stand only so long as the prop remains and Vietminh acquiescence in its survival can be obtained.[3]

Partly because of the pressures exerted by the lobby and by Senator Mansfield, the Eisenhower administration had been persuaded by October 1954 to override its earlier doubts as to supporting Diem. In a letter to the Vietnamese premier, Eisenhower affirmed American support for the Diem regime, but with certain conditions:

> The purpose of this offer is to assist the government of Vietnam in developing and maintaining a strong, viable support, capable of resisting attempted subversion or aggression through military means. The government of the United States expects

that this aid will be met by performance on the part of the government of Vietnam in undertaking needed reforms. It hopes that such aid, combined with your own continuing efforts, will contribute effectively to an independent Vietnam endowed with a strong government. Such a government would, I hope, be so responsive to the nationalist aspirations of its people, so enlightened in purpose and effective in performance, that it will be respected both at home and abroad and discourage anyone who might wish to impose a foreign ideology on your free people.[4]

Eisenhower's letter revealed the nature of the United States' commitments to Diem during the 1950s; social and political reforms were expected. The president agreed, subject to some stiff conditions and understandings, to provide economic and military assistance, including military advisors, material, and training. Initially, the U.S. military role was limited. Until the spring of 1960, the United States had stationed only 327 military advisors there; after May 1960, this number was increased to 685.

The administration translated its commitment to Diem into more decisive actions shortly after Eisenhower's letter was written. In mid-November, the president's special ambassador, General J. Lawton Collins, announced in Saigon that the United States would give "every possible aid to the government of Diem and to his government only." It would not consider "training or otherwise aiding a Vietnamese army that does not give complete and implicit obedience to its premier"[5]; this move was aimed at the commander of the army who was Diem's chief rival at this time. Ultimately American pressure put on Bao Dai led him to dismiss Diem's rival from his position.

In the period 1954–55, Diem had proven to be an effective leader. He successfully waged war on a number of local warlords operating in South Vietnam. These were semi-autonomous local fiefdoms, with private armies numbering in the thousands, and presenting a challenge to the central government. Binh Xuyen bandits controlled the Saigon police and openly defied Diem. Two armed religious sects, the Cao Dai and the Hoa Hao, were in constant revolt. Pro-French elements, hostile to Diem, ran the military and the civil service. By the end of 1955, Diem had defeated all of these groups, and would now be emboldened to attempt the ouster of the head of state, Bao Dai.

Basically serving as a puppet for the French in Vietnam, Bao Dai had been appointed head of state in 1950. Previously, he had served as the emperor of the Annam region of the country. He was described as introverted and given to moods of depression and indolence. Lacking any

VI. The Quiet Years

charisma or leadership skills, he was unlikely to challenge the French or to rally the Vietnamese around him.

In the spring of 1955, the next phase of the Vietnamese power struggle occurred when Bao Dai tried to check Diem's consolidation of power by summoning him to France (where he was residing) for probable dismissal. By now, the Eisenhower administration's earlier hesitation about backing Diem had been largely dissipated by his success in stabilizing conditions in Vietnam. In the following year, Diem would be able to replace Bao Dai as supreme leader of the country.

Leading Democrats shared the administration's partiality for Diem. In the Senate, Hubert Humphrey joined Senator Mansfield in voicing strong Democratic support, stating: "Premier Diem is the best hope that we have in South Vietnam. He deserves and must have the wholehearted support of the American government and our foreign policy. He is the only man on the political horizon of Vietnam who can rally a substantial degree of support of his people. If we have any comments to make about the leadership in it, let it be directed against Bao Dai. If the government of South Vietnam has not room for both of these men, it is Bao Dai who must go."[6]

With the United States so strongly behind him, Diem defied the orders of Bao Dai who was about to remove him from office, and with American encouragement, took steps to remove the emperor from his position as head of state. In October, Diem organized a referendum where people were asked to choose between him and Bao Dai. Historian George Kahin wrote that although he probably would have defeated the former emperor in an honest election, Diem ignored the counsel of his American advisers who felt that a reasonable margin was sufficient and would make a better appearance; instead he conducted a grossly unfair election in which he claimed the total of 98.2 percent of the vote.[7]

By the end of 1955, Diem had defeated challenges from the army, the various sects in Vietnam, and the emperor Bao Dai. His only remaining internal challenge was the most difficult—Ho Chi Minh and his Communist supporters. Also at this time, all remaining French influence was ended. France was strongly opposed to Diem, and with his rise in influence, and under U.S. pressure, it now withdrew all its forces from Vietnam. This troubled nation, firmly under Diem's control, was now solely a concern of the United States.

The administration was not challenged on its Vietnam policy. Political developments in the United States resulting from the 1954 congressional elections actually had helped President Eisenhower immensely. The Democratic victory in these elections resulted in the strengthening of executive control over American policy. The new leaders of Congress, Sam Rayburn in the House, Lyndon Johnson and Walter George in the Senate, plus others with long experience in foreign affairs, quickly extended the administration greater freedom in policy formulation than it had previously enjoyed from the Republican-dominated Congress. These men believed that extensive cooperation between the parties and the branches of the government was a requisite for national unity and effective policy.

This uncritical devotion of leading congressional Democrats to the Eisenhower administration became obvious in January 1955, when they granted approval for the president's Formosa resolution. This resolution gave the president wide-ranging powers to defend both Formosa (Taiwan) and several small islands off the coast of mainland China. Communist China had been threatening these islands which implied a threat to Taiwan itself. The entire debate in Congress lasted less than a week, that in the Senate less than three days. This pattern of support would be a forerunner of support for the president's overall Indochina policy.

Ironically, several members of Congress raised the argument that the president was infringing on his own constitutional powers by bringing the resolution before Congress. Senator Thomas Hennings of Missouri expressed his misgivings lest "the great historical powers of the presidency be in any way limited for future generations." Nor did Congress demand to know for what it was to be held jointly responsible under the resolution. One senator summed up the vagueness of the resolution by observing: "We gave the president authority that we don't have to give for the purpose of doing something that we are by no means agreed we want to do. And we did it in the name of national unity."[8] In this manner, a significant step in presidential control of foreign policy was taken in a casual and unconcerned manner.

In the Vietnam situation, as in the Formosa crisis, the administration's policies were generally unimpeded by the Senate. In the summer of 1955, Diem publicly stated his opposition to holding the elections slated for July 1956 under the terms of the Geneva Accords. Dulles supported this decision, stating he doubted whether free elections could be held in North Vietnam. (Yet Diem had rigged the 1955 referendum which ousted Bao Dai, claiming 98.2 percent of the vote.) The *New York Times* also defended

VI. The Quiet Years

Diem's decision, declaring, "We must not be trapped in a fictitious legalism that can condemn 10 million free people into slavery."[9]

It is not clear who sabotaged the 1956 elections, Diem or the United States. *The Pentagon Papers*, written by government officials during the 1960s, do not reveal the answer. Press coverage of the period created a strong implication that Diem, a staunch nationalist and anti–Communist as well as an independent operator, took this action with the later acquiescence of the United States. Historian George Herring wrote that the United States was leery of these elections almost as soon as they were agreed upon.[10] The evidence indicates that Diem opposed the elections, regardless of the American position. To the great relief of the United States, neither the Soviet Union, nor Communist China, registered a major protest to this development. Fears of a Korean-type invasion were not realized.

The ouster of Bao Dai and the cancellation of the 1956 elections apparently improved the prospects for the Diem regime. Senator Mansfield, reporting on his 1955 trip to Vietnam, noted: "There is today a reasonable chance of the survival and development of a free Vietnam. It has been gained largely through the dedication and courage off Ngo Diem." Mansfield went on to say: "As for our policies respecting Vietnam, they have effectively served the interests of the United States during the past year." Mansfield then cited what was probably the main reason for a strong backing of the Diem regime. "By furthering the cause of a free Vietnam, it may well have reduced the danger of the direct and costly involvement of our military forces in Southeast Asia." Therefore, he concluded, "there appears to be no need for major readjustments in our present policies respecting Vietnam."[11]

The lack of democracy in South Vietnam did not lessen U.S. support for Diem. Secretary Dulles was satisfied that Diem was competent and anti–Communist. Democracy was personally alien to Diem. His system of governing was called by one observer, "democratic, one man rule." He was described as having an authoritarian and Mandarin philosophy of government. Instead of a representative democracy, he set up a family dictatorship. Three of his brothers served in his cabinet of six. One of them, Ngo Dinh Nhu, an especially powerful figure in the government, was in charge of security operations. Another brother, Ngo Dinh Thuc, served as a Catholic cardinal. The youngest brother, Ngo Dinh Can, was a warrior chieftain in central Vietnam.

Bystanders to the Vietnam War

Diem's crushing of his opponents made his position in South Vietnam very strong by 1955. Later that year, Senator Humphrey warned against any reversal of United States policy toward Vietnam. Specifically linking Vietnam to the domino theory, he warned that "to lose South Vietnam will be to lose a strategic area of the world. Indonesia may be next. If South Vietnam falls, every country in the corridor of Southeast Asia will be in more difficulty, and we shall not be able to stop it."[12] Clearly Vietnam was being linked to the wider struggles of the Cold War.

By 1956, the American policy toward Vietnam had taken the essential character which it would retain throughout the decade. Assistant Secretary of State for Eastern affairs, Walter Robertson, in June 1956, described this policy in the following terms: "to support a friendly non–Communist government in Vietnam and to help it diminish and eventually eradicate Communist subversion and influence. To help the government of Vietnam establish the forces necessary for internal security. To encourage support for a free Vietnam by the non–Communist world."[13]

Diem's Senate support at this time was very strong. Senator Mansfield wrote in describing the Vietnam situation:

> If Diem continues to pursue the building of a free nation in South Vietnam with the same perceptiveness, courage and sure handedness which he has so far displayed, he will be ready for elections on unification when conditions for a free choice exist in Vietnam. Will the Vietminh be willing to accept them at that time? It is doubtful, but if they do, it is likely to be Ngo Dinh Diem's picture that will go in the ballot box and Ho Chi Minh's that will be cast into the dust.... In short, Diem's star is likely to remain on the ascendancy and that of Ho Chi Minh's to fade—because Diem is following a course which more closely meets the needs and aspirations of the Vietnamese people.[14]

Mansfield's optimistic comments describing Diem as the "wave of the future," sadly were not to prove true in the years ahead.

Another of Diem's early champions, Senator Kennedy, also reaffirmed his support for South Vietnam, whose survival he regarded as vital to the United States. He claimed that Vietnam represented

> the cornerstone of the free world in Southeast Asia, the keystone to the arch, the finger in the dike. Burma, Thailand, India, Japan, the Philippines and obviously, Laos and Cambodia are among those whose security would be threatened if the red tide of communism overflowed in Vietnam.... Vietnam represents a proving ground of democracy in Asia. The United States is directly responsible for this experiment—it is playing an important role in the laboratory where it is being conducted. We cannot afford to permit that experiment to fail.[15]

VI. The Quiet Years

Kennedy also declared:

> Vietnam represents a test of American responsibility and determination in Asia. If we are not the parents of little Vietnam, then surely we are the godparents. We presided at its birth, we gave assistance to its life, we have helped to shape its future. And if it falls victim to any of the perils that threaten its existence, then the United States, with some justification, will be held responsible, and our prestige in Asia will sink to a new low.[16]

Having described the American stake in Vietnam, Kennedy declared the United States had a vital mission to fill.

> What we must offer them is a revolution—a political, economic and social revolution far superior to anything the Communists can offer—far more peaceful, far more democratic and far more locally controlled.... We must assist the inspiring growth of Vietnamese democracy.[17]

The situation in South Vietnam seemed to be getting better at this time. Things were relatively quiet in the country, and the economy was apparently improving. This was in contrast to the major problems in North Vietnam at the time. Although politically unified behind Ho Chi Minh, its economy was deeply troubled. A land reform program had gone particularly badly. Nor was it getting aid from its Communist allies, Russia and China, who were not then involved in the Indochina quagmire.

In agriculture, the situation was especially serious. The war had devastated rice production in the north, always the poorer, less fertile half of the nation. Traditionally, the north had made up its food shortages by importing rice from the south. At this time, Saigon had halted all trade with the north, including food exports. Problems in the north obviously enhanced the prospects for South Vietnam.

Early in 1957, Senator Mansfield delivered in the Senate the first perceptive, non-euphoric analysis of the potential trouble in Southeast Asia. The senator referred to an unstable status quo which he called "this calm, this outward calm, this questionable calm, hanging by a tenuous truce, ... that has been presented to the people of the United States as an achievement of peace."[18] He queried: "How long will the calm last? Will the urge to unification in Indochina soon put an end to it?" There were forces of change in Asia that must be recognized. Mansfield went on to say:

> We do not even begin to have adequate insight into these and other important questions concerning the Far East. Yet, in that region no less than elsewhere and in some ways more, the forces of change are constantly at work. We shall be in a position neither to understand them not to deal with them if the people of this country

are lulled into a false sense of security about the Far East. The need is neither for a seeming calm nor a curtain of silence. The need is for facts, facts which the administration alone can supply. It is the need for action based on these facts, action designed to strengthen security and peace as they may be threatened in the Far East, not only for the moment but for years to come.[19]

Yet this warning went unheeded as evidenced by the euphoria manifested during Diem's 1957 visit to the United States. By this time, Diem seemed to have crushed the Communists in his country. In salvaging South Vietnam from the disorder that has threatened its existence, the *New York Times* reported that President Diem had "carved a deep niche in official esteem in Washington." Diem was regarded as one of the personal bulwarks against Communist encroachment in Southeast Asia.

The prime purpose of the trip was to demonstrate the depth of the administration's liking for him and what he had done. The sentiment was made clear by Eisenhower's remark at his news conference that Diem was a "truly, very great" leader and "staunch patriot" who had shown "courage and statesmanship in developing his government and country."[20] The *Christian Science Monitor* interpreted Diem's warm welcome as a sign that the United States was backing Diem and South Vietnam to the hilt.

These sentiments were also shared by other leading senators. Mansfield, despite his words of caution on the situation in Southeast Asia, regarded Diem as the "savior of all Southeast Asia." Senator Javits called Diem "one of the real heroes of the free world."[21]

The press was equally complimentary to the South Vietnamese leader. The *Washington Post* noted that "under [Diem's] skillful guidance and with substantial aid from the United States, Vietnam has obtained a stability that discourages adventuring." The *New York Herald Tribune* called Diem both "a leader of a free people and a statesman." The *Christian Science Monitor* called Diem a "stalwart champion of freedom." The *New York Times*, also enthusiastic in its descriptions, attributed Diem's warm welcome to the few triumphs of the United States in Asia since V-J Day and to a belief that the march of communism in Asia had been stopped.[22]

Not all the good news from Vietnam proved to be accurate. The economic reports of progress in South Vietnam failed to discuss the unbalanced nature of its economy. By 1961, South Vietnam was the fifth largest recipient of U.S. foreign aid. Between 1955 and 1961, U.S. aid to South Vietnam exceeded $1 billion, more than 78 percent in the form of military

VI. The Quiet Years

aid. While the standard of living was higher in the south than in North Vietnam because of the massive U.S. aid, did this indicate real economic progress? There was a distinct lack of infrastructure and growth; instead, much of the economic gains merely reflected an abundance of consumer goods, especially in Saigon. Almost none of this pointed to economic gains for the vast majority, 90 percent, living in the agricultural countryside. This lack of economic progress would later be defended in the notable comment by General Maxwell Taylor: "We should have learned from our frontier forebears that there is little use planting corn outside the stockade if there are still Indians in the woods outside."[23]

A major problem in the foreign aid program was also revealed that year. Senator Russell Long reported that through manipulation of the official currency, of $240 million given to South Vietnam, South Vietnam received about $75 million worth of benefits, and the import dealers picked up the benefits from the other $165 million. This scandal was merely a prelude to other foreign aid scandals in Vietnam which became more widely publicized in Washington later in 1959.

Although Diem's support remained strong in the United States, there was an explicit request for a closer look at Southeast Asia in Senator Mansfield's speech of May 1958. The senator reiterated his earlier warning of the potential danger in the three divided lands in Asia: China, Korea, and Vietnam. He claimed that "what exists in the Far East is no peace at all; it is a truce, a tenuous truce, patched together largely by unenforceable cease-fire agreements." Mansfield cited the urge for unification as a major problem in Vietnam, and claimed that unless there was some promise of progress toward its fulfillment, there would be no reasonable assurance of a durable peace. He feared "a mad resort to military action for unity" in Vietnam would "inevitably" draw the great powers into the struggle.[24] The senator's recommendation was to maintain the present tenuous truce, but at the same time pursue by peaceful means, the unity and full independence of Vietnam. Specifically, Mansfield called for gradual social and economic intercourse between the divided zones to pave the way for peaceful unification. He concluded by warning: "Let us not delude ourselves with the belief that what we now have is peace in Vietnam, and let us not delude ourselves with the belief that we are going to get peaceful unification and full independence in these countries by the policies we are now pursuing."[25] The *New York Times* added a footnote to the "deceptive calm" described by Senator Mansfield by noting that official reports indicated the Communists had been murdering local officials at the rate of about 28 per month.

Mansfield suggested a "Nehru Doctrine" as a political guide for Indochina. He felt the neutrality policy of Indian prime minister Nehru offered the best solution for the region. He regarded India as basically pro–Western, even if not overtly so. This enabled it to avoid Cold War problems, and would be a valuable model for Diem to follow. Mansfield hoped that Diem would bring democracy to South Vietnam as Nehru had done in India.[26]

The following year, more problems in the foreign aid program, rather than Mansfield's warning, led to widespread attention being given to United States policy in Vietnam. The reaction to this scandal indicated the resiliency of the American commitment to Vietnam. Amid charges concerning "outrageous scandals" in the Vietnam foreign aid program, a Senate Foreign Relations subcommittee headed by Senator Mansfield authorized Senator Albert Gore to go to Vietnam, accompanied by Senator Gale McGee of the Finance Committee. Both senators returned with upbeat assessments of the Vietnam situation. Gore concluded that the aid program had "many good features and worthy accomplishments," but also "some basic faults and irregularities." Even more positive, Senator McGee said the aid program was "soundly conceived and soundly executed."[27]

Despite some concerns over the aid program, U.S. policy remained unchanged. The 1960 Senate investigation concluded that the program had been of major benefit to both South Vietnam and the United States. The report issued by the Senate investigators said that many of the past abuses and flaws in the program could be traced to faulty supervision and regulation by the U.S. International Cooperation Administration. Praising the present administration of the program, Gore said he was "very pleased" to note the very strenuous efforts of United States officials in Vietnam to remedy error.[28]

Later in 1960, President Eisenhower reaffirmed that there would be no reversal of America's aid program to the Diem government. In a letter to Diem, Eisenhower said: "I want to assure you that for so long as our strength can be useful, the United States will continue to assist Vietnam in the difficult, yet hopeful struggle ahead."[29] The foreign aid scandals had not affected U.S. policies toward that nation.

A more serious problem had arisen with the substantial increase of terror activities in the south. In 1959, the North Vietnamese government

VI. The Quiet Years

had decided to strongly support the insurrection in the south, leading to an increase in the number of kidnappings and assassinations of government officials. In 1960, U.S. officials in Saigon were described as thoroughly alarmed by the crisis in Vietnam.

The reasons why the United States steadily maintained its support for Vietnam are similar to those behind its initial support; South Vietnam was regarded as a vital area to be withheld from the Communists. Although unwilling to go to war over Vietnam five years earlier, Eisenhower, in 1959, proclaimed to the American people the necessity to save Southeast Asia. The emerging countries of Asia and Africa had become the new focus in the Cold War struggle.

Senate Majority Leader Lyndon Johnson agreed: "The Communists long ago realized that the destiny of mankind could be settled in Asia." Senators Kenneth Keating and John Sparkman called South Vietnam's survival "an outstanding example" for the United States mutual security program. Senator Fulbright, who had previously made virtually no public comment on the problem, cited the earlier Senate report regarding foreign aid scandals and stated: "Yet despite many handicaps, Vietnam not only exists but it gives every promise of continuing to exist.... It would indeed be a carping critic who would find fault with the dimes when the dollars have accomplished so much."[30]

U.S. support for South Vietnam continued throughout the decade. The United States now had a "sink or swim" policy with Diem. He was regarded as the best leader the United States could expect in South Vietnam. Despite the autocratic nature of the Diem regime and substantial corruption uncovered in the U.S. aid it received, South Vietnam had not only survived but was also solidly pro–Western in an area of the world where the United States had few allies. This was enough to keep the U.S. Senate's support. Few senators truly understood the fragile nature of the Diem regime.

By 1960, the Vietnam problem had undergone a full cycle. In 1954, the situation was regarded as hopeless. The following year, American officials began to speak of "Diem's miracle." By 1960, clearly a crisis atmosphere existed, leaving a major problem for the new Kennedy administration.

VII

The Kennedy Years

During the nearly three years of the Kennedy administration, the United States steadily increased its commitment to Vietnam. This trend was not the result of a carefully reasoned policy. Because of the numerous other crises preoccupying the administration in its first two years, the Vietnam problem did not gain widespread public attention until 1963. Only in the closing days of his presidency did Kennedy belatedly realize that he had given this problem too little attention. Congress, too, had neglected the Vietnam problem due to the distraction of numerous other crises during this chaotic period, and its usual tendency to defer to the executive in periods of crisis. It had little direct impact on the course of American Vietnam policy during the Kennedy years.

The *Pentagon Papers* indicate the almost negligible role played by Congress in the formulation of Kennedy's Vietnam policy. Early in his presidency during the Laotian crisis, Congress was wary of a possible military involvement in Southeast Asia. In November 1961, the *Pentagon Papers* reported: "President receiving static from Congress; they are against using United States troops."[1] When this crisis was "settled" through an international conference, Congress thereafter remained aloof from Southeast Asian affairs for nearly the duration of the Kennedy administration. The *Pentagon Papers* do not report on the relation of Congress to presidential decision-making on this matter during most of the Kennedy administration. Only during the turbulent days of 1963 did Senate interest grow noticeably. Because of the overall limited involvement of the Senate, Kennedy did not regard the Congress as a inhibiting factor in the formulation of his Vietnam policy.

A number of factors impelled the executive branch to escalate the nation's commitment to South Vietnam in 1961. The Kennedy administration's vacillating and compromising position regarding the Cuban and

VII. The Kennedy Years

Laotian crises in that year as well as Soviet leader Nikita Khrushchev's threat to push the Berlin question convinced the president that he must stand firm in Vietnam. This problem became more urgent when in 1961 the Soviet Union stepped up its efforts in the Third World, including Vietnam. After the Bay of Pigs debacle in Cuba, Kennedy concluded he could not accept another foreign policy defeat in the same year and maintain his credibility. "I can't take a 1954 defeat [referring to the French defeat at Dien Bien Phu] today," he declared. While Eisenhower could have blamed the French or colonialism for a defeat in 1954, he lacked those assets.

Furthermore, the additional conventional forces Kennedy advocated during his 1960 presidential campaign were now available and encouraged him to take a strong stand in Asia where it was felt they would be most effective in deterring communism. Kennedy had been critical of Eisenhower's "New Look" defense strategy, severely limiting the level of U.S. ground troops. Ironically, one of the factors causing Eisenhower not to intervene in 1954 had been the conclusion of the Ridgeway Report that U.S. conventional forces were thin and their commitment to Vietnam would have exposed American interests elsewhere.

As the Communist threat in Vietnam grew more serious in 1961, the Kennedy administration took a number of steps which involved the United States deeply in what became the Asian quagmire. At his press conference on May 5, Kennedy revealed the dilemma which faced him. He was reluctant to send combat troops to Southeast Asia, declaring, "In the final analysis, the South Vietnamese have to—and we cannot do it for them—they have to organize the political and social life of the country in such a way that they maintain the support of their people. There is a limit beyond which our efforts cannot go."[2] Yet, at the same time, he announced that one of the purposes of Vice President Johnson's upcoming trip would be to study the possibility of assigning United States forces to South Vietnam. Johnson returned from his visit with recommendations for a determined effort to save Southeast Asia, and South Vietnam in particular. Kennedy acted upon these recommendations by authorizing a substantial increase in United States advisory and training personnel in South Vietnam. Simultaneously, he agreed to bolster that nation's army by 20,000 men.

The very limited public reaction in Congress to the administration's Vietnam policy at this time generally took the form of supporting or encouraging a strong position. In June, Senator Fulbright indicated his support of the administration's hints that the United States might have to intervene with its own forces in Vietnam. The senator expressed his willingness to aid the Saigon regime because it apparently was willing to defend itself. Fulbright's support was notable since he had opposed both the Cuban intervention and a proposed Laotian intervention in 1961. This new position was ironic since he became a leading critic of intervention in Vietnam after 1965.

Shortly afterward in a speech to the Senate, Fulbright clarified his Vietnam position Describing the Diem regime in modestly favorable terms, he stated:

> [This regime] has been courageous and diligent in bringing order and progress out of the chaos that attended the country's birth. It can point to a record of steady accomplishments.
>
> Yet the regime has lacked something in benevolence and has shown impatience for the people who have suffered a great deal.... It is a regime that of necessity has been authoritarian, but one that also has been perhaps unnecessarily severe. On balance, however, it should be said that the accomplishments of this regime are overlooked by many observers and commentators who all too frequently have accepted uncritically the most abusive gossip and propaganda circulated about president Diem and his administration.
>
> The term "qualified success" could be used to describe the American performance in Vietnam, as well as the Diem regime.... For the United States, the proper course is to continue sustaining and supporting efforts of the Vietnamese Army to cope effectively with the Communist guerrillas while devoting at least as much effort to assisting and guiding the Vietnamese people in their struggle for dignity and economic independence.[3]

Senator Thomas Dodd of Connecticut also supported the growing American commitment to South Vietnam, although in more affirmative and confident tones. In that same month, he declared:

> If the United States, with its unrivaled might, with its unparalleled wealth, with its dominion over sea and air, with its heritage as the champion of freedom— if this United States and its free world allies have so diminished in spirit that they can be laid in the dust by a few thousand primitive guerilars, then we are far down the road from which there is no return.
>
> In right and in might, we are able to work our will in this question. Southeast Asia cannot be lost unless we will it to be lost; it cannot be saved unless we will it to be saved.[4]

In this general atmosphere of congressional acquiescence, if not encouragement, in a bolder Vietnam policy, Kennedy acted to build up American influence. At a SEATO meeting later that year, American offi-

VII. The Kennedy Years

cials said the United States would not "tolerate another Laos," a reference to the crisis that ended with a conference at Geneva, but with no solution. In October, Kennedy dispatched General Maxwell Taylor and Professor Walt Rostow to investigate the situation in Vietnam. In another move, Kennedy called General James A. Van Fleet back from retirement to assist the U.S. Army in training specialists in guerrilla warfare. General Van Fleet headed the United States military mission in Greece in 1947 when President Truman launched the Truman Doctrine policy to save Greece from Communist rebels. The *New York Times* interpreted these two assignments as a possible move to assist South Vietnam in the same way that the United States helped the Greek government quell the Communist rebels after World War II.[5]

Upon his return from Vietnam, General Taylor urged a determined effort, utilizing American forces, to save South Vietnam. He proposed the introduction into Vietnam of more than 10,000 regular American ground troops, and accepting the possibility that as many as six full divisions (approximately 100,000 soldiers) might eventually be required. The mission of these American troops would be to guard against invasion from the north by regular North Vietnamese divisions and to man the northern borders against infiltrators, while the South Vietnamese dealt with the guerrillas in the rear. Kennedy agreed to accept the general concept stressed by both the Taylor and Johnson reports, that a determined effort be made to save South Vietnam, although he refused to dispatch American combat troops at this time.

Historian Arthur Schlesinger, Jr., an adviser to the president, stressed Kennedy's strong reluctance to commit United States combat troops in

President John Kennedy with leading advisors Defense Secretary Robert McNamara (*left*) and General Maxwell Taylor, who urged strong support for South Vietnam (JFK Presidential Library).

1961, as recommended by the Taylor report. In November, he told Schlesinger: "They want a force of American troops, They say it's necessary in order to restore confidence and maintain morale. But it will be just like Berlin [a reference to his sending a small number of additional troops there in 1961]. The troops will march in; the bands will play; the crowds will cheer; and in four days, everyone will have forgotten. Then we will be told we have to send in more troops. It's like taking a drink. The effect wears off and you have to take another."[6] Schlesinger attributed the president's limited actions at this time to his great confidence in General Taylor's judgment (although deferring on committing U.S. troops) as well as the need to counter the Russians' obstinate position on Berlin, their unwillingness to negotiate a nuclear test ban, and their overall belligerent attitude. Furthermore, former State Department official Roger Hilsman noted there was a distinct absence of feasible alternative policies to pursue in South Vietnam.

The Kennedy administration's desire to carry out, with increased aid, this country's commitment to Vietnam was officially conveyed in a public exchange of letters between presidents Kennedy and Diem on December 15, 1961. By the end of the year, American personnel in Vietnam numbered over 2,000, going beyond the limit of 685 that was set in the Geneva Accords.

In early 1962, Vietnam became a more partisan political issue in the Senate. This reflected concern over the obvious buildup of forces. On February 8, the administration established a new military command in South Vietnam and named a four star general to head it; a primary purpose being to demonstrate the United States' determination to prevent a Communist takeover. (Only once before, in Greece during the late 1940s, had a United States military aid mission been commanded by a full general.) This command was created on the recommendation of General Taylor.

The Republican attack on this buildup took the form of a call for more information from the administration. On February 13, the Republican National Committee called on President Kennedy to make a full report to the American people on the United States' involvement in the fighting in South Vietnam. In its publication *Battle Line*, the committee charged that the president had been "less than candid" in his comments on the extent of United States involvement in South Vietnam. The publication raised the question whether the United States was "moving toward another Korea" which might embroil the entire Far East. The article added

VII. The Kennedy Years

sardonically": the people should not have to wait until American casualty lists are posted before being informed about the real nature of the nation's commitment to South Vietnam."[7]

Democratic Senator Mansfield, the majority leader in the Senate since 1961, responded almost immediately to these partisan charges. From early 1961 to February 1962, he noted there had been at least 50 meetings covering American involvement in Vietnam. Of these, at least the 40 had been between representatives of the Departments of Defense and State with Congress. Therefore, Mansfield declared, Congress had actually had a "surfeit of information" on the situation. He then cautioned Congress not to tread on the executive's responsibilities in foreign affairs, stating:

> We have got to be careful as to the constitutional line of demarcation between the prerogatives and responsibilities of the president and those of the Congress in connection with this matter. It is the president's responsibility to decide and to act. It is ours to advise as we are able in our individual and collective wisdom, and to the extent that it it is constitutionally required, to consent.... I hope that this effective collaboration and mutual accommodation will continue, because it is essential for the welfare of the nation that they continue. But they will not continue if partisans on one side insist that Congress has no concern in these matters or if partisans on the other side insist that Congress should look over the president's shoulder 24 hours a day and to tell him how to conduct the foreign policy of the United States. That is the president's responsibility.... It is in the nation's interest that he is supported exercising it. It will be a disservice to the nation and hence, to any party, to impede him, for whatever reason, in exercising it.[8]

This call to respect the president's judgment and defer to him on Vietnam was later reversed when Mansfield became a leading critic of President Johnson after 1965.

Generally throughout the remainder of 1962, the Vietnam issue was superseded by other crises, particularly the Cuban crisis. There was but scattered public debate in the Senate over the Vietnam issue, and so diverse was its nature that it could not guide the administration's handling of the problem. In March, Senator Humphrey declared his support for maintaining South Vietnam's independence from that "greatest risk": Communist aggression, Communist conquest, and Communist advance. Yet he ambivalently added that the United States' role must be limited in this endeavor. Humphrey noted with satisfaction, however, that Kennedy's action in Vietnam had the "full and concurrent support from members of Congress on both sides of the aisle."[9]

Humphrey's stress on the stakes in South Vietnam was seconded by

Bystanders to the Vietnam War

Senator Dodd who sensed a possible catastrophe for the United States in that part of the world. While not clearly defining his ultimate course of action, Dodd stated that "if the Communists ever succeeded in establishing their dominion over the whole of Southeast Asia, a possibility if South Vietnam should fall, they will, in effect, have cut the world in half.... The Communist conquest of Southeast Asia would produce so serious a shift in the world balance of power that our very ability to survive would be called into question."[10]

By the summer of 1962, there were a few voices being raised as to the true situation, rather than to vague cataclysmic generalizations. Senator Mansfield declared the United States was following a "mark-time course," and that events were "moving toward a point of critical decision."[11] He was now wavering on his former deferential attitude. His Republican colleague, Senator Gordon Allott, questioned Defense Secretary Robert McNamara's continued glowing reports of progress. "I wonder just what Mr. McNamara means by progress.... I wonder if the secretary knows what is going on. The conflicting reports about the situation in South Vietnam are, to say the least, somewhat confusing. Secretary McNamara says things are 'going well' there. Yet news dispatches from qualified and able observers in that area report an altogether different story.... Just who was being misled? Is it Mr. McNamara; or is it the news observers? Or are the American people being misled by the administration?"[12]

These Vietnam critics were drowned out by the surfacing of other world crises as well as an apparent improvement in the military situation in Vietnam during the year. Undersecretary of State Roger Hilsman reported that the influx of United States military aid and advisers had boosted the previously languid efforts of the South Vietnamese forces. Several key indicators of military progress—number of enemy killed, number of government desertions, number of enemy weapons captured, number of enemy defections, and the number of government-initiated actions—seemed to indicate the war effort had markedly improved over the previous year. In January 1963, President Kennedy announced to the Congress that "the spearhead of enemy aggression in South Vietnam has been blunted." As a reflection of the optimism felt toward the Vietnam situation at this time, Schlesinger quotes Kennedy as declaring early in 1963: "I regard Latin America as the most critical area in the world today."[13]

Yet there were troubling developments which cast doubt over these optimistic sentiments. Most of the countryside in South Vietnam was

VII. The Kennedy Years

under the "influence" of the Communist insurgents. Even the reports of military progress came into question. A clear indication of the situation occurred on January 2, 1963, when Diems's government suffered an embarrassing military defeat. In the battle of Ap Bac, a Communist force of approximately 200 inflicted significant losses on a government force of about 2,500, and then managed to escape.[14] By the end of the year, the war seemed to be in a downward spiral.

During 1963, senatorial attention to and criticism of the Vietnam problem grew steadily more intense. The origin for the criticism which buffeted President Johnson's Vietnam policy so vehemently can be seen during the debates of the last year of Kennedy's administration. Earlier in the year, Senators Morse and Mansfield sounded cautious advice to the president, while their more aggressive colleagues, Jackson and Symington, urged a hard line toward the Southeast Asian Communists. Vietnam was clearly becoming a more critical foreign policy issue.

At the request of President Kennedy, senators Mansfield, Claiborne Pell, and Alexander Smith and Representative Haley Boggs toured Vietnam in late 1962. In February 1963, Senator Mansfield, leader of the four-man Senate investigating team, reported his findings. The study warned that the struggle in Vietnam was fast becoming an "American war" that could not be justified by present United States security interests in the area. It called for "a thorough reassessment of our overall security requirements on the Southeast Asia mainland" with a view to the orderly curtailment of United States aid programs. The report questioned whether the $5 billion spent in aiding Southeast Asia since 1950 has been justified by the results. It was even more doubtful about the wisdom of continuing present policies indefinitely. But it recommended "extreme caution" in cutting back the current level of military and economic aid to Southeast Asia as well as congressional restraints in an area of exclusive presidential discretion.

Recalling his previous visit to Vietnam seven years earlier, Mansfield voiced his deep concern over the trend of events during the interim. "What is most disturbing is that Vietnam now appears to be, as it was then, only at the beginning of coping with its grave inner problems," he said. Regrettably he added: "All of the current difficulties existed in 1955 along with the hope and energy to meet them, but it is seven years later and $2 billion of United States aid later. Yet substantially the same difficulties remain if, indeed, they have not been compounded."[15]

Bystanders to the Vietnam War

The chief concern of the report was the prospect that intensification of United States support of the Vietnam central governments could only end in the conversion of the struggle into an "American war."

> This intensification inevitably has carried us to the start of the road which leads to the point at which the conflict could become of greater concern and greater responsibility to the United States that it is to the government people of South Vietnam.
>
> In present circumstances, pursuit of that course could involve an expenditure of American lives and resources on a scale which would bear little relationship to the interest of the United States or, indeed, to the interests of the people of Vietnam.
>
> If we are to avoid that course, it must be clear to ourselves as well as to the Vietnamese where the primary responsibility lies in the situation. It must rest with the Vietnamese government and people. What further effort may be needed for the survival of the republic in present circumstances must come from that source.
>
> If it is not forthcoming, the United States can reduce its commitment or abandon it entirely, for there is no interest of the United States in Vietnam which would justify, under present circumstances, the conversion of the war in that country primarily into an American war to be fought primarily with American lives.[16]

Prominent hawks such as senators Jackson and Symington took a less cautious viewpoint of the problem. Jackson stated the absolute necessity for victory in Vietnam, declaring, "The Communists have got to be stopped where they make their effort. There isn't any nice, pleasant battleground where we could make a stand in preference to this one."[17] Symington was willing to take a risk to achieve such a victory, suggesting the possibility of either bombing or invading Hanoi.

Senator Mansfield was quick to comment on these early pressures to deepen the United States commitment. "I would say to the advocates of extension of the Vietnamese conflict that to call for what looks like an easy and cheap way of doing the job in Vietnam is to advocate a long step towards another Korea."[18]

One of Diem's most important initiatives, his program to solve the security problem in the countryside, added to the Vietnam quagmire. To protect the rural population, the government adopted the strategy of strategic hamlets. Much of the local population was relocated to heavily fortified villages, forced to abandon their ancestral homes, with heavy financial losses. These hamlets, each surrounded by a moat and ringed with a barrier of sharpened bamboo, resembled medieval castles. The program, begun in 1959 to exclude Viet Cong infiltrators and abandoned as a failure in 1963, ironically made it easier for Communist insurgents to gain more support in the countryside.

VII. The Kennedy Years

In late spring, the United States role in Vietnam became the subject of intense controversy when the Diem regime became embroiled in a dispute with the Buddhists. On May 8, Diem's troops fired into crowds protesting orders forbidding the display of flags on the anniversary of Buddha's birth. When Diem refused to conciliate the Buddhists, additional protests broke out. On June 11, the Buddhists shocked the world when an elderly monk burned himself to death on a main street in Saigon. Failing to gain any satisfaction from the Diem regime, the protests quickly spread.

In late August, the Buddhist crisis seriously deteriorated. On August 21, Diem's special forces conducted a series of massive raids on the Buddhists in various cities, arresting more than 1,400. These raids now raised serious consideration to the possibility of replacing the Diem regime. Assistant Secretary of State Roger Hilsman stated: "We could not sit still and be the puppets of Diem's anti–Buddhist policies."[19]

American criticism of the anti–Buddhist raids led Diem's brother, Ngo Dinh Nhu, to suggest that the number of Americans in Vietnam was excessive, and hinting of a possible deal with Hanoi. President Kennedy, while declaring the immediate necessity for them to remain, expressed the hope that withdrawals could "perhaps" begin at the end of the year. These raids on the Buddhists were to begin a sustained period of tense relations between the United States and South Vietnam.

As relations with Diem grew steadily cooler throughout the rest of the year, American policymakers found themselves in a dilemma. One American official in Saigon explained by saying: "Diem knows he's got us hooked, and he knows we know he's got us hooked."[20] The lack of a strong alternative to Diem and the unknown to be expected should Diem be toppled put the United States in a bind, and in the constant hope that Diem would reform. Therefore, on July 9, in a personal letter to the Vietnamese leader, President Kennedy reaffirmed the United States support for the South Vietnamese regime.

Relations with Diem became much worse following a series of extraordinary protests by the Buddhists. Over a period of several months beginning in June, seven Buddhist monks publicly burned themselves to death, actions which captured the attention of the world. The callous reaction by Diem and his family only inflamed the affair even more intensely.

The situation had become unstable in late August following a series of government raids of the Buddhist pagodas. These raids and the accompanying mass arrests led to widespread criticism from both the Congress and President Kennedy. In an extraordinary television interview on September 2, Kennedy condemned the policies of the South Vietnamese government and called for a complete reform in Saigon. He said that country's leaders should realize that the war against the Communist guerrillas was "their war" and that it could not be won unless the government recovered the popular support it had lost. Kennedy declared: "We are prepared to continue to assist them, but I don't think that the war can be won unless the people support the effort and in my opinion, in the last two months, the government has gotten out of touch with the people. In the final analysis, it's their war. They are the ones who have to win it or lose it. We can help them, give them equipment, we can send our men out there as advisors, but they have to win it, the people of Vietnam, against the Communists."[21] President Kennedy added his belief that there was still time for the government to regain the support of the people but only if there were" changes in policy and perhaps with personnel" (referring principally to Diem's powerful brother and sister-in-law, Ngo Dinh Nhu and Madame Nhu).

The president made it clear, however, that he did not agree with those who advocated a withdrawal of United States troops and aid from South Vietnam. "That would be a great mistake," he said. "I know people don't like Americans to be engaged in this kind of effort.... But this is a very important struggle, even though it is far away."[22]

Kennedy had long stressed the importance of Vietnam, "the cornerstone of the free world in Asia." Years earlier, he had attacked Truman for "losing" China. He was sensitive to the possibility of losing Vietnam, and the political fallout that would follow. According to historian George Herring, he was "less willing than Truman and Eisenhower to permit the fall of Vietnam to communism."[23]

Throughout the early fall months, Congress and the president debated over the utility of cutting aid to the Saigon regime in order to spur reforms. The president was obviously reluctant to take such a step, declaring, "It would not be helpful at this time" to reduce United States aid. He feared that cutting aid would lead to a collapse of the South Vietnamese government. "Strongly in our minds," the president said, "is what happened in the case of China at the end of World War II, where China was lost—a weak government became increasingly unable to control events. We don't want that."[24]

Opinion in the Senate was becoming more openly hostile to the Diem regime. Senator Frank Carlson stated: "Our nation cannot continue the intolerable and indefensible position it presently occupies in South Vietnam." Senator Birch Bayh charged that supporting Diem was "a complete contradiction of our concepts of personal freedom and individual liberty." Some senators went further and urged an American withdrawal from the quagmire in South Vietnam. Senator Morse advocated an American pullout if its allies will not share the commitment. Senator George McGovern stated outright and unconditionally that "the United States' position in Vietnam has deteriorated so drastically that it is in our national interest to withdraw from that country our forces and our aid."[25]

In mid–September, the Senate openly expressed its increasing distaste for the events in Vietnam through Senator Church's resolution, urging that further American aid be terminated and American personnel withdrawn if cruel repressions were not stopped. Introducing the resolution, Church made an extremely sharp attack on the Diem regime.

> The Diem regime in South Vietnam has adopted policies of cruel repression. We have been dismayed by its persecution of the Buddhists, by the desecration of their temples, and by the brutality of attacks upon them. Too horrified to look, we have turned our eyes away from the sacrificial protests of Buddhists monks burning themselves alive in the streets of Saigon. Such grisly scenes have not been witnessed since the Christian martyrs marched hand-in-hand into the Roman arenas.
>
> We have been denounced by the very members of the ruling family we have helped to keep in power. To persist in the support of such a regime could only serve to identify the United States with a cause of religious persecution, undermining our moral position throughout the world.[26]

Yet despite these sharp protests, the Senate generally remained deferential to the executive. Senator Thomas Kuchel bespoke a sentiment held by many, stating: "The responsibility for the crisis in South Vietnam is one which runs to the President of the United States. It seems to me that this is a time when a crisis is brewing and when the responsibility rests, not in the Senate, but in the White House, and the State Department, and in the representation which this government maintains in South Vietnam."[27]

The Church resolution actually fitted in with this viewpoint, serving as an aid rather than a threat to the administration's policy. There was no immediate vote on the Church resolution because the administration preferred to keep it as a lever in its negotiations with Saigon. The St. Louis *Post-Dispatch* reported that the Senate would not pass the resolution should the administration not favor such a move. One purpose of the resolution was demonstrated when Ambassador Henry Cabot Lodge warned Diem that congressional pressures at home might force the administration to end all aid to his regime.

Pressure from Church's resolution had a limited effect. Senator Church told the Senate of "the first encouraging reports to come out of Vietnam in many weeks," citing the lifting of press censorship and martial law in Saigon, the rescheduling of legislative elections and the release of imprisoned Buddhist monks. Yet it was soon clear that Diem had decided not to accede to the key American demand, to dismiss his brother. The American response remained uncertain, eventually taking the form of a limited aid cut off.

Resisting these pressures, Diem reminded the United States that "we are not a protectorate." Besides being an independent-minded leader possessed with an uncompromising attitude toward outside advice, Diem's stubbornness might be somewhat attributable to the United States' overindulgence toward him. In mid–1962, Homer Bigart wrote in the *New York Times*: "In the last 15 months, a parade of VIPs, starting with Vice President Johnson and ending with the recent visit by Defense Secretary McNamara, regaled Mr. Diem with promises of all the help you need. Hearing his leadership lauded as an 'irreplaceable asset,' the president presumably assumes he could reject any proposals he disliked and still get all the money and military equipment you want to from his friends in Washington."[28]

In November, events took a dramatic turn with the assassination of Diem and his brother Nhu, and their replacement by a military junta. While not directly involved, the United States government had clearly created the atmosphere that made the coup possible. The *Pentagon Papers* indicate that the Kennedy administration was aware of the projected November coup, had encouraged it, and had done nothing to stop it. Nevertheless, the *Papers* exonerate the administration from direct complicity in the coup, or in the assassinations of Diem and Nhu, which it opposed.[29]

In the Senate, there was a cautious response to the coup. Senator Mansfield linked his regret over the death of Diem with a call "for a reassessment and reappraisal of our policy in South Vietnam and in all of Southeast Asia." He added: "One would hope that the people of South Vietnam will obtain the kind of government out of these tragic developments which will be responsive to them. It remains to be seen whether such a government shall emerge, and any reappraisal of our policies would

VII. The Kennedy Years

be a factor of the utmost importance."[30] Senator Burke Hickenlooper said the developments posed "a very serious situation that will require scrutiny and watchful waiting until we know more about it." Senator George Aiken was cautious about the United States' role in the coup, stating: "If we are at all involved, we don't want another failure. I hope we don't have another Bay of Pigs on our hands."[31]

Except for these comments of caution, confusion, and sometimes outrage, the interest and impact of Congress on the policy during the Kennedy years was negligible. Aside from the Foreign Relations Committee, the Senate paid very little heed to Vietnam. Former assistant secretary of state for congressional relations, Frederick Dutton, noted that from 1961 to the summer of 1963, "Congressional interest is pretty nearly zero. Inquiries about Vietnam never reach 10% of the inquiries about Cuba."[32] Then, from July to October 1963, White House and State Department mail on Vietnam was 34 percent of the total volume of mail from the public. Even though there was a sudden great public interest in the macabre, it never led to strong public attempts to influence policy. The burnings created a wave of revulsion in the United States against the Diem government, but very little pressure on either congressmen or diplomats to do anything about them. Unlike when dealing with Cuba or Russia, policy decision-makers had a great deal more freedom to deal with Vietnam in general and the Buddhist crisis in particular.

In assaying his final decisions about Vietnam, Kennedy, through deference and disinterest by both the public and Congress, had virtually a free hand on Vietnam. His main preoccupation was his own indecision. At the time of his death, no definite exposition of his all policy had ever been handed down.

What Kennedy would have done had he lived is a subject of much speculation among scholars and laymen alike. Several authoritative sources have stated either that Kennedy had not decided what his ultimate policy would have been or that there is no way of knowing what he would have done. The *Pentagon Papers* and political analysts Kahin and Lewis' *The United States in Vietnam* stated that it is impossible to know what Kennedy would have done in Vietnam. Ted Sorenson's book, *Kennedy*, declared that Kennedy never formally made a decision in order not to bind himself or to allow his critics to charge him with weakness. Historian Arthur Schlesinger, Jr., implied that Kennedy, at the time of his death, realized that his Vietnam policy had failed, that it required more study, but failed to say what new directions the Kennedy policy would have taken.³³

A different point of view was expressed by the president's former advisor Kenneth O'Donnell. He stated that sometime in 1963, Kennedy had decided (largely on the advice of Senator Mansfield) to withdraw from Vietnam. O'Donnell said that Kennedy's announcement in October 1963, that 1,000 American troops would be withdrawn by the end of the year, fitted into his unannounced policy to pullout of Vietnam. The *New York Times*, interviewing several of the people cited by O'Donnell, including Senator Mansfield, implied that O'Donnell's thesis was correct.³⁴

Yet Roger Hilsman's *To Move a Nation* and the *Pentagon Papers* suggest that the 1,000-man pullout was based on faulty intelligence; and that the United States realized how bad the situation actually was only after the coup against Diem took place.³⁵ This factor implies that the withdrawal policy may have been reversed even if Kennedy had lived; neither stated that the withdrawal was part of a reversal in policy.

Therefore, until more information is available, Kennedy analysts must base their thesis upon the slain president's political record, especially his nearly three years in office. The evidence suggests that Kennedy was inclined to be cautious toward committing American combat troops, and that ultimately, like Eisenhower in 1954, he would refuse to intervene militarily. Throughout his House and Senate career, Kennedy had consistently stressed the nationalist elements in Third World political struggles; consequently, he warned of the danger of converting the struggles into white men's colonial wars. He continued to incline toward this viewpoint as president.

Presidential advisor Ted Sorenson wrote of the sobering effect which the Bay of Pigs fiasco had had upon Kennedy, and led him to be more cautious in resorting to military solutions to complex diplomatic problems, particularly with regard to the use of American troops. Sorenson also stated that Kennedy never forgot the advice of General Douglas MacArthur, given in 1961, warning him against the commitment of American soldiers on the Asian mainland. In addition, Sorenson declared that in 1961, at the time of the Taylor report, all of Kennedy's principal advisors favored the commitment of substantial numbers of American troops, only to be overruled by the president.³⁶ The *Pentagon Papers* report that during the intense debate of fall 1961, Kennedy refused to accept, as recommended by his advisors, the unqualified commitment to the goal of saving South

VII. The Kennedy Years

Vietnam from communism.[37] In this context, Kennedy's continual stress during his years in office of South Vietnam's own responsibility for its survival may be the key to what his ultimate policy would have been.

The above factors clearly denote Kennedy's skepticism over committing American combat troops to Southeast Asia, even when urged to do so by virtually all his major advisors. Perhaps Kennedy's 1963 speech at American University provides the clue—his call for an end to the old myths, for an accommodation with the Communists, and a recognition that there could not be an American solution to every world problem.

VIII

The Tonkin Gulf Affair

In the period immediately preceding the Tonkin Gulf affair, the executive continually hinted at greater involvement in Vietnam. The withdrawal deadline of October 1965, was quietly dropped. Parallel to the more aggressive position of the executive was a shift in the Senate's public sentiments. The strong opposition voiced in the fall of 1963 gave way to more "hawkish" sentiments and acquiescence in the president's increasingly bolder stands. Only senators Morse and Gruening expressed strong and open opposition to this increasing commitment to Vietnam. Repeatedly, they urged the Senate to assert its constitutional authority in foreign affairs.

In August 1964, the Senate passed the Tonkin Gulf Resolution. Reservations as to the implications of the resolution were voiced but because of the crisis, the Senate refused to challenge the president's foreign policy prerogatives. Generally, the entire period before the Tonkin Gulf crisis was one in which the Senate exhibited little public concern over Southeast Asia; this reflected the plethora of domestic matters being considered by the Senate at that time.

President Johnson stated his determination to stand firm in Vietnam as soon as he assumed office. In late 1963, he declared: "I am not going to be the president who saw Southeast Asia go the way China went."[1] In a new year's message to the head of South Vietnam's military regime, Major General Duong Van Minh, Johnson pledged a flow of military aid and personnel "as needed to assist you in achieving victory" over Communist guerrillas. The president's letter also opposed neutralization of South Vietnam, an idea which he regarded as only "another name for a Communist takeover."

Historian Eric Goldman noted that Johnson's determined position may have reflected his particular approach and background in foreign

VIII. The Tonkin Gulf Affair

Senator Ernest Gruening, one of two senators to vote against the Tonkin Gulf Resolution (U.S. Senate Historical Office).

affairs. He stressed Johnson's position that the United States had to show it was strong in the world, and that it would oppose aggression. He was a believer in unilateral American solutions to world problems. Most significantly, Johnson was too anxious to apply the "Munich" analogy to diplomatic problems.[2] His more aggressive attitude in 1963 was in sharp contrast to his more cautious position at the time of the 1954 Dien Bien Phu crisis.

By late 1963, Vietnam seemed about to become a major foreign policy disaster. By now, Senator Mansfield had little hope for a possible U.S. military victory, and no faith in the military junta which had replaced Diem. Unlike President Johnson who looked at a military solution, Mansfield aimed at a negotiated solution. He backed Charles DeGaulle's August 1963 call for a new Geneva Conference to solve the Vietnam problem.

Johnson's views took on more serious overtones as the administration began to stress the ever-growing danger of a collapse in South Vietnam. In December, Defense Secretary Robert McNamara informed the president that unless the policy changed, Vietnam would collapse within 60 to 90 days. In testimony before the House Armed Services Committee the following month, McNamara disclosed that the situation in Vietnam "continues grave" and reported that the Communists had made considerable progress since the coup against the Diem regime the previous November. McNamara expressed hope that the withdrawal program could continue, but added that the United States might have to intervene with "all necessary measures within our capability." At his news conference on February 1, President Johnson declared he saw no chance then of negotiating a peace for South Vietnam, and pledged instead a greater effort in the guerrilla war.

Bystanders to the Vietnam War

The administration's hints of a greater involvement led to the reopening of the Senate debate on the Vietnam question, although with only a limited number of participants. On February 19, Senator Mansfield urged the Johnson administration to encourage, rather than spurn, French efforts to negotiate with Communist China for the neutralization of Southeast Asia. A major commitment of American lives to the ten-year-old war was not justified, Mansfield added. The United States should therefore welcome a negotiated settlement. Americans should ask, after weighing the national interest and the probable cost in lives and resources of a war in Vietnam, whether they preferred the uneasy neutrality in Laos and Cambodia to a possible long, drawn-out war.[3]

The Republican wing of the Senate demonstrated at this time the "hawkish" stand it would assert with increasing intensity in the crucial summer months. Senator Goldwater declared that the United States must either "win or withdraw" from South Vietnam and blamed President Johnson for the way "things are falling apart around the world."[4]

Senator Jacob Javits also took a firm position, declaring: "The present position in Southeast Asia is only insurance against a future which seems so foreboding in terms of the intentions at the moment which Communist China declared and reiterated for so very long." He believed it was important to stay in South Vietnam and do the job, though it was costly and difficult.[5]

As the Vietnam crisis seemed to worsen by March, the Senate debate began to attract more participants. Senator Kenneth Keating repeated an earlier request for a full congressional review of the war in South Vietnam and the role of the United States in it. He was

Senator Barry Goldwater, a leading "hawk" on Vietnam and Republican presidential candidate in 1964 (courtesy Marion Trikosko).

VIII. The Tonkin Gulf Affair

more cautious about a major escalation. "It is our obligation, as citizens and as elected representatives, to call upon outside experts, as well as the government spokesmen who have heretofore monopolized information in this conflict."[6]

Further indications by the administration of plans for an impending escalation in Vietnam caused particularly strong comments by Democratic senators Morse, Gruening, and Dodd. Senator Gruening was especially critical. On March 10, President Johnson was called upon by Gruening to withdraw American forces from what he characterized as "this bloody and wanton stalemate. The time has come to cease the useless and senseless losses of American lives in an area not essential to the security of the United States. This is a fight which is not our fight, into which we should not have gotten in the first place. The time to get out is now, before the further loss of American lives. I consider the life of one American worth more than this putrid mess. I consider every additional life that is sacrificed in this forlorn venture a tragedy. Some say, if the sacrificing continues, it will be denounced as a crime."[7]

His leading ally in opposing Johnson, Senator Wayne Morse, similarly called for withdrawal in equally strong terms. In a Senate speech, he asserted: "We have always regarded Southeast Asia to be beyond the perimeter of United States defense. Southeast Asia is not essential to the United States defense. Southeast Asia may very well be essential to the defense of some of our allies, but where are they? They ran out on us. We should never have gone in. We should never have stayed in. We should get out."[8]

However, one of the president's main supporters strongly differed. Senator Thomas Dodd, replying to Morse and Gruening in a speech on March 11, deplored what he called "the querulous, faint-hearted chorus of those who always asks the price of victory. We must help turn the war against North Vietnam, the home base of the aggressor. The United States should be willing to assist the South Vietnamese to open a sustained guerrilla operation in North Vietnam and give the Communists a taste of their own medicine."[9] Dodd would maintain this "hawkish" position throughout the Johnson years, and would be one of the president's strongest allies in the Democratic Party.

For the most part, Republicans had kept out of the fray on the Senate floor at this time, although several took a notably hard position. Campaigning in New Hampshire and California, future 1964 Republican presidential nominee Senator Barry Goldwater, maintained that victory, rather than mere containment of the Communist Vietcong, should be the United States' stated goal. To reach this goal, he suggested that air and naval strikes against North Vietnam might be advisable. Another Republican "hawk," Senator Margaret Chase Smith, added: "We should either pull out and stop losing our men over there or we should go in and clean up."[10]

Yet there was no overall consensus as to how to proceed. The Senate's Republican leader, Senator Dirksen, deplored the situation in Vietnam as evidence of the lack of a clearly defined administration position for dealing with Communist aggression throughout the world. However, he conceded that he had no specific solution to propose.

Among the most influential Democrats, public opposition was generally nonexistent. Senator Fulbright, later a leading critic, basically supported the Vietnam policy as "the wisest at the moment under very difficult circumstances." He did not think withdrawal could be realistically considered under present circumstances, declaring:

> It is difficult to see how a negotiation, under present military circumstances, could lead to termination of the war under conditions that would preserve the freedom of South Vietnam. It is extremely difficult for a party to a negotiation to achieve by diplomacy objectives which it has conspicuously failed to win by warfare. The hard fact of the matter is that our position is at present a weak one; and until the equation of advantages has been substantially altered in our favor, there can be little prospect of a negotiated settlement which could secure the independence of a non–Communist South Vietnam. Recent initiatives by France, calling for the neutralization of it, have tended to confuse the situation without altering it in any fundamental way.[11]

In a defense of the president, he stated:

> It seems clear that only two realistic options are open to us in Vietnam in the immediate future: expansion of the conflict in one way or another, or renewed effort to bolster the capacity of the South Vietnamese to prosecute the war successfully on its present scale. The matter calls for thorough examination by responsible officials in the executive branch; and until they have had an opportunity to evaluate the contingencies and feasibilities of the options open to us, it seems to me that we have no choice but to support the South Vietnamese government and army by the most effective means available. Whatever specific policy decisions are made, it should be clear to all concerned that the United States will continue to meet its obligations and fulfill its commitments with respect to Vietnam.[12]

Although Fulbright was a later critic of the president, his views were aligned with President Johnson at this time. He rejected the French suggestion of

VIII. The Tonkin Gulf Affair

a neutral Vietnam. He also rejected negotiations until the U.S. military position was stronger. He declared: "We are committed and it would be disastrous to withdraw."[13] Fulbright added his belief that "senators spouting off didn't help the situation." He preferred that his fellow Democratic senators communicate their ideas privately to President Johnson instead of engaging in public debate.

In late March, the administration decided to continue its policy of massive aid to South Vietnam; it rejected at this time a deeper American involvement or negotiated withdrawal. Rather than promise a projected date of withdrawal, the administration promised help for "as long as it is required."

The situation in South Vietnam became unsettled when General Nguyen Khan replaced General Dong Minh as head of the government. He seemed to offer a more determined effort in the war than his predecessor. (He too would be ousted a year later when he hinted at a neutralization policy for South Vietnam; his ouster paved the way for the "Americanization" of the war.)

In a speech on March 26, Secretary McNamara announced that the administration rejected "withdrawal," "neutralization," or "peace at any price" in the Vietnamese war. He reaffirmed the plans of the United States to accelerate military and economic support for the newly installed Khan regime. The possibility of direct military action against North Vietnam to curb the supply of arms and military leadership to the Vietcong guerrillas, he left open. His theme was that the United States planned to remain in the struggle until an "independent and stable country there made it safe to withdraw." In closing his speech, McNamara warned that the situation in South Vietnam "has unquestionably worsened since last fall."[14] The *Pentagon Papers* state that the administration had quietly approved guerrilla actions against North Vietnam on February 1, 1964. McNamara was implying publicly what had been decided nearly two months earlier.[15]

Despite the worsening situation in Vietnam, the Senate debates on this issue continued to be dominated by a small number of participants. Morse and Gruening remained the most vociferous senators in opposition to the policy, and decried Congress' lack of initiative in asserting its foreign policy powers. In a major Senate speech intended as a rebuttal to McNamara's earlier speech, Morse said that the Johnson administration "must be repudiated" unless it abandons the policy of supporting what he called the "McNamara war in South Vietnam." The United States, Morse declared, "couldn't be more wrong" in what he called its unilateral intervention. He warned that McNamara was "holding out the possibility of expanding the fighting into North Vietnam and even into China itself."[16]

The senator charged that the United States policy in Vietnam was doomed to failure. In additional speeches throughout the following months, Morse kept up his attacks on the administration. The senator claimed that the United States' participation in the war in Vietnam was "illegal and a menace to the American nation. Aside from the illegality of our action there is the sheer stupidity of a unilateral American land war in Asia whose only promise is to bog us down there indefinitely."[17]

Morse went on to challenge the Senate's role, declaring: "You [the Senate] cannot run away from this policy question. You will have to stand up and be counted, whether you want to or not, because the people of this country will count you." Noting McNamara's pledge to Saigon to give it whatever aid was needed "forever," Morse reacted: "In the absence of a treaty, in the absence of a joint resolution, in the absence of some other form of law, the secretary of defense or even the president cannot make such a pledge and have it carry the weight and the meaning of law. Such a pledge by the secretary of defense does not, and cannot, commit the American Congress to anything."[18]

Senator John Sparkman countered Morse with a contrary view of the proper role of the Senate on Vietnam, and on all foreign policy questions. In a major defense of executive power, the Alabama senator declared: "As to foreign policy, I have often stated that the person charged under the Constitution with the responsibility of pronouncing and carrying out the foreign policy of the United States is the president of the United States, and that he cannot escape that responsibility."[19]

Sparkman went on to compare the situation in Vietnam with the 1947 crisis in Greece and Turkey. He noted that President Truman did not try to escape his responsibility during that crisis. "He [Truman] announced that as a foreign policy that we were going to support Greece and Turkey, and that we were going to take over the burden that Great Britain was no longer able to carry. He asked Congress for funds sufficient to do the job, and announced that it was his purpose to send military helpers. They were sent. I have often wondered why we could not carry out some such program as that in Vietnam."[20]

While the debate was heating up, the administration intensified the discussion when it was reported on May 15 that Secretary McNamara had

VIII. The Tonkin Gulf Affair

laid before President Johnson a new plan for increased military and economic support for South Vietnam. The situation in Vietnam was obviously deteriorating at this time. In a very controversial suggestion, the secretary added this might involve sending more American troops. To implement this suggestion, President Johnson alerted the congressional leaders of both parties to the strong possibility that he would seek increased economic and military assistance for that beleaguered nation. He apparently was preparing the Senate for bolder policies in Southeast Asia. So grim was McNamara's description of the situation that Senator Leverett Saltonstall commented "it looks like a long and tough pull in South Vietnam."[21]

Congress indicated it would back the president when it favorably responded to his new aid request for an extra $125 million in economic and military aid for the war against the Communist guerrillas in South Vietnam. This money was in addition to the appropriation of about $500 million already sought by the administration for programs in Vietnam for the next fiscal year.

Senator Morse immediately expressed his opposition to the new aid proposal. As in the past, Morse was the most vocal critic of the president's new move for Southeast Asia. Morse stated: "The president should be seeking to send to the Congress, instead, a proposal for a declaration of war. The president of the United States should not be sending to the Congress a subterfuge proposal, a policy of intention, a policy of carrying on a war by executive action rather than by congressional action."[22] Once again, Morse was virtually a lone voice in challenging the president. Countering Morse's "dovish" position was the hard line being urged upon the president as the Republican Party came out for "victory" in Vietnam. On May 25, Senator Goldwater made the startling suggestion that low yield atomic weapons could be used to defoliate the forests along South Vietnam's border to expose the jungle supply lines of the Communist-led rebels. He also urged the bombing of bridges, roads, and railroads used for bringing supplies from Communist China and North Vietnam unless the Communists halted military shipments over them.

Other Republicans lined up to support his hardline position. The final report of the Republican task force on "American strategy and strength" stated for Vietnam

> the United States must make a full-scale commitment to halt Communist China's military expansion and subversion in Asia and the Pacific. The victory in South Vietnam over the military and subversive threats of communism is urgently

Bystanders to the Vietnam War

required. We must repeal today's complacent commitments to prevent a Communist victory and substitute a commitment to ensure a victory for freedom. And once Southeast Asia is free to pursue the development of democratic institutions of its own choice, the United States should then be prepared to help stabilize the area and to protect it from the Communist virus.[23]

By the summer of 1964, administration supporters in Congress accepted intervention, if necessary, if all else failed. The Johnson policy had gathered considerable support in the Senate. Senator Humphrey warned against a coalition government. Senator Sam Ervin urged "victory" in Vietnam. Senator Javits believed young Americans would gladly give their lives to save Vietnam. Only senators Morse and Gruening urged an immediate withdrawal from Vietnam.

By this time, President Johnson seemed publicly to be leaning toward this "hawkish" position. Leading congressional authorities were told by the president of plans to carry the war to the north, through intensive bombing and a possible blockade of the North Vietnamese coast. In late June, President Johnson said that the United States, when necessary, would not hesitate to risk war to preserve the peace. He appeared to be delivering another in a carefully prepared series of statements designed by the administration to convince Communist China that the United States would go to war rather than see Southeast Asia overrun.

While the Republicans and the administration seemed to be taking a harder line, most senators, especially the Democrats, were undecided on the problem. A typical reaction was voiced by Senator George Aiken. Though opposed to an escalation of the war, Aiken declared: "Where does the responsibility rest for deciding what course our country should follow relative to the Southeast Asia problem? The responsibility rests squarely and heavily on the shoulders of the president of the United States, and the correctness of his decisions will determine his place in history."[24] Agreeing with Aiken, there was a general tendency to go along with the president from such prominent later doves as senators Church, Fulbright, Pell, Cooper, and Javits.

Throughout July, the situation grew more tense. On July 1, Secretary Rusk warned that peace could not be obtained by "acquiescence to aggression" by Communists in South Vietnam and Laos. In mid–July, the administration announced it was sending an additional 300 of its special forces to Vietnam, thus reversing the withdrawal trend of the previous fall. By the end of the month, the United States announced it was sending an addi-

VIII. The Tonkin Gulf Affair

tional 5,000 men to Vietnam. This move was not challenged by Congress, reflecting Johnson's efforts in June and July to assure Senate leaders that he opposed a wider war. The president's assurances had won him the support of such important senators as Mansfield, Fulbright, Russell, and Stennis.

In view of Congress' tendency not to assert itself in the preceding months, it was not at all surprising that Congress completely deferred to the president's wishes during the dramatic days of August 1964. On August 2, an American destroyer reported being attacked by North Vietnamese gunboats in international waters, and having sunk one of the attacking ships. No casualties or damage to the destroyer was reported. Two days later, the United States again claimed that a destroyer had been attacked in international waters, once again without suffering casualties. (The second incident was questionable; the ship's captain saying afterward he was not sure an attack had actually occurred.) Following the second reported incident, Johnson authorized an American bombing attack on North Vietnam.

After the two incidents in Tonkin Gulf, President Johnson asked Congress to assent to a broadly worded resolution, agreeing to his military response against North Vietnam, and to allow him to act in the future to protect American interests in Southeast Asia. *New York Times* writer Tom Wicker later reported that President Johnson had carried a copy of the resolution with him for months, waiting for an opportune moment to present it.[25]

The circumstances surrounding the two incidents later became a matter of controversy. The administration at first claimed the destroyer Maddox just happened to be in the area with no specific mission. Later it was revealed that the destroyer was assisting the South Vietnamese conduct a guerrilla operation in the area. Regarding the second incident which provoked the U.S. bombing response, many would later conclude it never actually occurred. It was based mainly on unreliable radar and sonar intercepts. Regardless of the actual circumstances of early August, this period helped propel the United States into a major escalation in Vietnam only six months later. Historian Anthony Austin questioned "whether a minor incident had been exploited by the president to implement a prior plan to send the bombers against the north and to obtain a resolution from Congress?"[26]

Congress reacted to the president's request with conflicting sentiments.

H. J. Res. 1145   PUBLIC LAW 88-408

Eighty-eighth Congress of the United States of America

AT THE SECOND SESSION

Begun and held at the City of Washington on Tuesday, the seventh day of January, one thousand nine hundred and sixty-four

Joint Resolution

To promote the maintenance of international peace and security in southeast Asia.

Whereas naval units of the Communist regime in Vietnam, in violation of the principles of the Charter of the United Nations and of international law, have deliberately and repeatedly attacked United States naval vessels lawfully present in international waters, and have thereby created a serious threat to international peace; and

Whereas these attacks are part of a deliberate and systematic campaign of aggression that the Communist regime in North Vietnam has been waging against its neighbors and the nations joined with them in the collective defense of their freedom; and

Whereas the United States is assisting the peoples of southeast Asia to protect their freedom and has no territorial, military or political ambitions in that area, but desires only that these peoples should be left in peace to work out their own destinies in their own way: Now, therefore, be it

Resolved by the Senate and House of Representatives of the United States of America in Congress assembled, That the Congress approves and supports the determination of the President, as Commander in Chief, to take all necessary measures to repel any armed attack against the forces of the United States and to prevent further aggression.

Sec. 2. The United States regards as vital to its national interest and to world peace the maintenance of international peace and security in southeast Asia. Consonant with the Constitution of the United States and the Charter of the United Nations and in accordance with its obligations under the Southeast Asia Collective Defense Treaty, the United States is, therefore, prepared, as the President determines, to take all necessary steps, including the use of armed force, to assist any member or protocol state of the Southeast Asia Collective Defense Treaty requesting assistance in defense of its freedom.

Sec. 3. This resolution shall expire when the President shall determine that the peace and security of the area is reasonably assured by international conditions created by action of the United Nations or otherwise, except that it may be terminated earlier by concurrent resolution of the Congress.

John W. McCormack
Speaker of the House of Representatives.

Lee Metcalf
(Acting) President pro tempore of the Senate.

APPROVED
AUG 10 1964

Lyndon B. Johnson

VIII. The Tonkin Gulf Affair

To some senators such as Allen Bible, George Aiken, and Allen Young, the integrity of the United States was at stake. Others such as senators George Smathers and Barry Goldwater believed the Communist aggressors must be taught a lesson, lest they be tempted to strike at American forces again. More cautious senators voiced concern as to the open-ended nature of the resolution which had been laid before the Congress. Only two senators, however, expressed outright opposition to the Tonkin Gulf Resolution, root and branch.

The resolution contained two parts. The first section endorsed the president's bombing of North Vietnam in response to the enemy attacks. The second section was the controversial blank check, authorizing the president to do whatever was necessary to preserve the peace and security of Southeast Asia.

Senator Morse represented the most extreme opposition to the president's Southeast Asia resolution. He claimed that the United States had actually provoked the attack upon its forces by provocative actions. American ships, he noted, were in the vicinity when South Vietnamese naval units launched an attack against North Vietnamese installations. Morse had been given secret information by a confidant in the Pentagon concerning these raids by the South Vietnamese navy. The *Pentagon Papers* fully reveal the espionage nature of the American vessels which the administration claimed were merely innocent bystanders in the Tonkin Gulf area.

Joined by his ally, Senator Gruening, Morse condemned the resolution as a "great mistake" which would subvert and circumvent the Constitution of the United States, particularly Article 1, Section 8 (the war-making clauses). "We are in effect giving the president of the United States war-making powers in the absence of a declaration of war." Gruening concurred, declaring the resolution to be nothing more than a predated declaration of war, not merely in South Vietnam, but it all Southeast Asia.[27]

At this time, Senator Fulbright stood firmly behind the president. Fulbright saw nothing unusual about the seemingly broad powers Congress had given the president. While conceding that the resolution gave the president authority to take the United States to war, he justified this as a response to new developments in the field of warfare. Fulbright stated: "In the old days, when war usually resulted from a formal declaration of

Opposite: A copy of the Tonkin Gulf Resolution (U.S. National Archives).

war—and that is what the Founding Fathers contemplated when they included that provision in the Constitution—there was time in which to act. Things moved slowly, and things could be seen developing. Congress could participate in that way. Under modern conditions of warfare, it is necessary to anticipate what may occur. Things move so rapidly that this is the way in which we must respond to the new developments. That is why this provision is necessary or important."[28]

One of the most powerful senators, Richard Russell of Georgia, also saw nothing unusual about the broad grant of power contained in the resolution. He cited as precedent other congressional resolutions passed during the Formosa crisis of 1955, the Lebanon crisis of 1958, and the Cuban crisis of 1962. Russell declared that no vital transfer of power was authorized by the resolution, although he did note that the resolution signified "that Congress shares in the determination that this country will do everything necessary to defend our national interests, wherever they may be endangered."[29]

Senator J. William Fulbright (*left*), early supporter and later extreme critic of U.S. policy in Vietnam, and Senator Wayne Morse, longtime critic of U.S. involvement in Vietnam (courtesy Warren K. Leffler).

VIII. The Tonkin Gulf Affair

Morse and Gruening, without belittling the power of the president to conduct the nation's foreign affairs, urged caution in the Senate regarding the resolution. Gruening reminded the Senate of its constitutional duty to "advise and consent; especially is this true when it is specifically called upon by the executive floor its participation in momentous decisions of foreign policy." Gruening added that "we in the Senate would be derelict in our duty if we did not individually express our views if these views embody doubt or dissent, and where a vote is called for, to cast that vote as our conscience directs."[30]

In more blunt terms, Morse urged that Congress not surrender its powers in foreign policy to the president. He decried the fact that the resolution gave the president the power to make war without a declaration of war.

> It feeds a political trend in this country that needs to be checked. For some time past in this republic, we have been moving in the direction of a government by executive supremacy.... It is dangerous to the freedoms and liberties of the American people to vest in any president, at any time, under any circumstances, power that exceeds the Constitutional concept of three coordinate and coequal branches of government.... In times of hysteria and high national emotionalism, it is only human for most people, particularly those not sitting in the seats of legislative responsibility, to be willing to look the other way on such questions as I raise in this debate against this again this year.[31]

Morse and several other senators feared that the resolution would lead to an American land war in Asia. During the debates, Senator Owen Brewster queried Fulbright: "Is there anything in the resolution that would authorize or recommend or approve the landing of large American armies in Vietnam or in China?" Fulbright replied: "There is nothing in the resolution that contemplates it, [although] the language of the resolution would not prevent it. It would authorize whatever the commander-in-chief feels is necessary."[32]

Senator Gaylord Nelson attempted to clarify the ambiguities surrounding the resolution by proposing an amendment, opposing a direct military involvement in the Southeast Asia conflict. The Nelson amendment was effectively thwarted by Senator Fulbright who responded: "I do not object to it as a statement of policy. I believe it is an accurate reflection of what I believe is the president's policy, judging from his own statements. That does not mean that as a practical matter, I can accept the amendment. It would delay matters to do so. It would cause confusion and require a conference, and present us with all the other difficulties that are involved in this kind of legislative action. I regret that I cannot do it, even though I do not at all disagree with the amendment as a general statement of policy."[33] His assurances of Johnson's intentions satisfied Nelson, who withdrew his amendment. Passage of this amendment might have altered Johnson's future actions in South Vietnam. Former Secretary of State Dean Rusk stated that its passage would have made it more difficult for Johnson to implement his policy of escalation.

Fulbright's response to the Tonkin Gulf Resolution indicated the dilemma of many senators. Later he admitted that he was influenced by partisanship. He was determined to do nothing which would affect Johnson's reelection prospects against Senator Goldwater whose election he regarded as a "disaster" for the United States. Fulbright also stated his belief that Johnson was a true "peace" candidate, and that he would not escalate the war in Vietnam. Furthermore, the senator's lack of a challenge to the president's foreign policy fitted in well with his oft-practiced policy, to leave the primary responsibilities and foreign policy to the president. It is difficult to determine what Fulbright's actual views on Vietnam were at this time; judged by his comments throughout the year, he seemed to be in agreement with the basic policies of President Johnson.

The debate in Congress on the proposed resolution for the defense of Southeast Asia demonstrated just how much the powers of the presidency had grown, and how those of Congress had declined in foreign affairs. Congress was asked to show its support for the president

Senator Gaylord Nelson, who unsuccessfully sponsored the Nelson Amendment that would have weakened the Tonkin Gulf Resolution (U.S. Senate Historical Office).

VIII. The Tonkin Gulf Affair

in a crisis; without hesitation, it did so. The Senate Foreign Relations and Armed Services Committees endorsed the resolution after perfunctory hearings, and with only one dissenting vote on August 6.

One odd light on the debate was the apparent apathy with which it was conducted. The *New York Times*, covering the first debate, reported "no atmosphere of impending crisis." The chamber was not even one-third full most of the time. Members entered, expressed their support of the resolution briefly, and left.

Afterward, Fulbright would state incredulously that the Foreign Relations Committee spent only one hour and 40 minutes in hearings on the resolution. The Senate hearings were a mere formality—so much so that Senator Dirkson wanted to dispense with them all together and send the resolution directly to the Senate floor. Such a move, however, would have required unanimous consent, impossible because of Senator Morse.

Historian Joseph Goulden explains the Senate's lack of initiative to its desire to nominate Johnson without embarrassment to him. He cited an unnamed senator as telling Morse at the time: "Hell Wayne, you can't get in a fight with the president at a time when the flags are waving and

President Johnson signing the Tonkin Gulf Resolution (U.S. National Archives).

we're about to go to a national convention. All Lyndon wants is a piece of paper telling him he did right out there, and we support him, and he's the kind of president who follows the rules and won't get the country into war without coming back to Congress. That's all it is—don't be so excitable."[34] After brief floor debates, the Tonkin Gulf Resolution was adopted by the Senate on August 7 Once the president had ordered the bombardments of the North Vietnamese coast and called publicly for a congressional resolution, authorizing him to use any military power he chose in defense of that area, the Congress could not deny his request without seeming to repudiate and weaken his handling of the emergency. The Congress was free in theory only. In practice, despite the private reservations of many members, it had to go along. Once the president had committed the nation to a course of action, the Congress had to comply; it had the choice of helping the enemy if it did not comply, which was no choice at all.

Various other explanations of the Senate's acquiescence to Johnson have been offered. In the spring of 1970, Morse stated that the Senate was over-obsessed with a fear of the Communist bogeyman in August 1964. Senator Gruening referred to the Senate's lack of courage. He called the Senate "spineless" for not asserting its foreign policy prerogatives. He stated: "If one were to write a book on the shortcomings of the Congress with respect to United States military involvement in Vietnam, he could entitle it: *Congress, The Spineless Branch*."[35]

Secretary of State Dean Rusk offered a more positive explanation of the Senate's "going along." He stated that criticism was muted throughout the pre–Tonkin Gulf period because of the political elections coming up, and also because the administration enjoyed "wide support" in Congress through 1965. He noted that Congress was "confused" about the Vietnam problem, and was "relieved" that President Johnson, rather than it, would have to make the vital decisions on Vietnam.[36]

IX

The Decision to Escalate

In the year that elapsed between the Tonkin Gulf incident and the decision to send large numbers of combat troops to Vietnam, the Senate played a deferential role as the crisis steadily worsened. Much of the Senate's lack of initiative stemmed from its failure to arrive at any consensus on Vietnam. With few exceptions, the general mood of the Senate was to let the president handle the crisis; most of the post–1965 critics of policy in Vietnam were silent at this time.

By September 1964, the crisis in Vietnam was getting worse. Approximately 18,000 American servicemen were stationed there with the total expected to reach 21,000 by the end of the year. The American death toll was approaching 300, with additional casualties almost a daily occurrence. The Saigon government controlled only about 30 percent of the country's territory, and the enemy's forces were estimated at about 50,000 guerrilla fighters in South Vietnam.

The situation in the fall of 1964 was confused by the American presidential election. During the campaign, President Johnson took a "dovish" position on Vietnam, although he carefully refrained from declaring that the United States would withdraw from the country.

In answer to suggestions by Senator Goldwater and others that the United States carry the war in Vietnam to the north, Johnson said: "Before I start dropping bombs around the country, I would think about the consequences of getting American boys into a war with 700 million Chinese. We're not going north and drop bombs at this stage of the game, and we're not going south and run out, and let the Communists take over either."[1]

By October, the Johnson administration was reviewing its policy in Vietnam. As South Vietnamese unity and military efficiency declined, the administration gradually began to restate its aims and to emphasize that "the United States regards as vital to its national interests and to world peace the maintenance of international peace and security in Southeast Asia." What started out as a limited commitment to play a subsidiary role gradually became a United States commitment, not only to maintain the peace and security of South Vietnam, but also the whole of Southeast Asia.

From the outset of his presidency, Johnson appeared more inclined to escalate than former presidents Eisenhower and Kennedy. He totally believed in President Truman's containment theory and President Eisenhower's domino theory. He also assumed a hard line toward the Communists would help him gain support for the Great Society, and feared a Republican assault on his domestic program if he lost Vietnam. Johnson remembered Truman's domestic program lost all Republican support after the fall of China to the Communists and the stalemate in the Korean War.

On November 1, 1964, shortly before the presidential election, the Communists attacked an air base at Bien Hoa, killing four servicemen and wounding 76.[2] Running as the "peace" candidate, Johnson chose not to respond. He will respond more aggressively to another attack on an American air base three months later after winning reelection by an overwhelming margin.

In late November 1964, there were indications of a move toward escalation by the Johnson administration. Ambassador Maxwell Taylor was now recommending to the president that airstrikes against certain targets in North Vietnam and Communist-controlled parts of Laos be employed. At the time, Johnson took no immediate military steps, preferring that the possibilities for developing a more stable civilian government in Saigon be explored before committing the United States to a wider war. In the aftermath of the Diem assassination the previous year, the political climate in South Vietnam was very uncertain.

A new dimension was added to the Vietnam dilemma the following month when Senator Frank Church urged a shift in American policy. He recommended neutralization of Southeast Asia as a proper objective for the United States, and suggested that a role be found for the United Nations as a guarantor of national boundaries in that area. Church said he hoped that the United States would never be forced to withdraw but, if it came to that, "we must be prepared for that possibility." Church opposed proposals for extending the Vietnamese war to North Vietnam. He said it was folly to believe that escalation of the war to the north would save the situation in the south. In addition, he expressed the belief that

IX. The Decision to Escalate

expansion of hostilities to the north would inevitably bring the Chinese Communist into the war.

Church did not underestimate the difficulty the Senate faced in seeking to redirect presidential policy, declaring: "It's especially hard for a free, popular government to change course. We have a tendency to oversell our policy with respect to any given country in such a way that public opinion hardens behind it, and then it becomes very difficult to change course."[3] Church was among a small emerging group of vocal Democratic critics of United States policy toward Vietnam. Along with Mansfield, he argued for considering neutralization proposals favored by President Charles de Gaulle of France. Another of these critics, Senator George McGovern, proposed a 14-nation conference to seek a political settlement in South Vietnam. What should the United States do if the plans for negotiations or neutralization fail? The dilemma surrounding all these critics, according to some observers, was that none had an alternative course to suggest that

Senator Mike Mansfield, who unsuccessfully tried to persuade President Johnson to avoid war in Vietnam, speaking with President Johnson (courtesy Frank Wolf).

did not involve the enormous risk of an expanded war or abandonment of all American commitments in the area.

The opposite point of view was adopted by Senator Dirksen, the Republican minority leader, who favored a hard line. Originally a "dove" in 1954, Dirksen now urged President Johnson to seek a "united decision" from congressional leaders of both parties on whether to fight or withdraw from South Vietnam. "A hard decision now has to be made," he said. His own review of decisions and precedents made it clear that, as commander-in-chief, the president could act on his own if he determined that there was a danger to national security. But he noted that in any such action, "the president, as have his predecessors, would want the declared support of national leaders, if not of Congress as a body." Dirksen then added: "To give up in Vietnam means a loss of face throughout the Orient. The rank of the United States would plummet. And from the standpoint of the Philippines and Guam, we would have no anchor point left."[4]

In December, Johnson sent Secretary McNamara to investigate the situation in Vietnam. The secretary reported the Communists controlled far more territory in South Vietnam than had been reported. He claimed Diem's strategic hamlet program had failed, and that South Vietnam might collapse in 60–90 days. McNamara's gloomy report encouraged Johnson to secretly approve bombing the Ho Chi Minh trail in Laos, to be followed by bombing North Vietnam. However, he was still hesitant on committing U.S. combat troops. The United States was moving closer to becoming a full participant in the war.

On the eve of the opening session of the 89th Congress in January 1965, Senator Mansfield predicted that a full-scale debate on United States policy in Vietnam would emerge, "and it would be a good thing." In the debate which ensued, however, there was such a diversity of opinion that no one position could be urged upon President Johnson as the advice of the Senate. Senator Aiken warned against expanding the United States commitment unless the nation was ready to face all-out war that would include nuclear weapons. Senator Mansfield concurred: "Expansion will not resolve the problem. It is more likely to enlarge it, and in the end, we may find ourselves engaged all over Asia in a full-scale war." Raising the specter of a new Korea, Senator Ellender said it was time for the United States to get out "without any ifs or buts."[5]

Other senators took a harder position. Senators Harry Byrd and Frank Lausche warned that neutralization would lead to Communist domina-

IX. The Decision to Escalate

tion. Offering the toughest formula, Senator Strom Thurmond said: "Give the South Vietnamese all the supplies they need to bomb the North Vietnamese and if necessary, bomb them with United States troops, planes and ammunition." Even the "dovish" Senator George McGovern noted the considerable support being voiced for a hard military line toward North Vietnam.[6] This lack of consensus in the Senate greatly limited its ability to shape Johnson's policies.

In early February, President Johnson took the fateful step that brought escalation when he ordered massive airstrikes on North Vietnam, allegedly as a response to a bloody Communist attack on an American base at Pleiku in South Vietnam. (According to prominent journalist Charles Roberts, the bombing program had actually, been unofficially approved several months earlier.)[7] In the Pleiku attack, seven Americans were killed and 109 were wounded. A few days later after another Communist attack on American soldiers' quarters, Johnson ordered even heavier bombing attacks. The United States had shifted from reprisals to a continued program of massive bombing of North Vietnam (operation Rolling Thunder). Since continued bombing would require many more U.S. troops and support personnel, the path to a major escalation in the war had been cleared.

At the time, the war in South Vietnam was not going well. General Khanh who had followed the first government to replace the ousted Diem regime, then led by General Minh, had himself proven to be an ineffective leader, both politically and militarily. That same month, the United States moved to oust the Khanh government which was hinting at a neutralization policy, totally unacceptable to the Johnson administration. Unfortunately, the situation only worsened after the change in government.

Johnson received the full support of congressional leaders of both parties for the retaliatory air strikes he ordered against North Vietnam. Aside from support voiced by the leaders, there was relatively little comment on his decision, and almost none of it was critical. Most members believed that the president must have congressional support in such a situation, whatever doubts or apprehensions they felt as individuals.

The massive bombing program after Pleiku proved to be a major escalation in the U.S. war effort. Its purpose was not only to deter future attacks, but also to strengthen South Vietnam's will to fight. Hopefully, it would hold off a collapse and raise morale in South Vietnam. One senator who opposed the new bombing policy was Senator Mansfield who feared it might provoke Chinese intervention.

Bystanders to the Vietnam War

The Vietnam issue soon became more heated amid rumors that the United States was about to expand its role in the war. Senators McGovern and Church called for negotiations to end the American commitment. McGovern said that military victory in Vietnam appeared impossible. Church declared that "systematic and sustained bombing of Vietnam, unattended by any offer of recourse to the bargaining table, can only lead us into a major war."[8]

On the other hand, other senators expressed strong support for the administration's policy. The Republican leadership stated that if there were any differences, "it is the belief that these measures might have been applied [earlier]." Advocates of a negotiated settlement were accused by leading Republicans of proposing to "run up the white flag" and of "a retreat to Pearl Harbor." Senator Dirksen stated that recent speeches advocating some form of negotiation had the ring of the truce talks of 1954 affecting Vietnam and of the Laotian agreement of 1962, both of which had disappointing results.[9]

By late February, the United States war commitment was clearly escalating. The administration tacitly acknowledged that it had changed the rules of American involvement, citing the Tonkin Resolution as authorization for the move. The use of American planes and crews on combat missions against the Viet Cong guerrillas had supplanted an earlier policy of having Americans "advise and assist" the South Vietnamese, and fight only in self-defense.

Congress' role in this decision on escalating the American commitment was minimal. Its views on Vietnam were being influenced by the president, and not the reverse, asserted Tom Wicker of the *New York Times*. He declared: "Certain speeches made recently in support of the administration may well have been inspired in the White House. It has not been uncommon for the administration even to furnish ideas and working drafts for such speeches."[10]

Wicker cited several reasons for Congress' weak position. The Tonkin Gulf Resolution had authorized the president to take whatever steps might be necessary to repel attacks on American forces and to assist any SEATO nation in defending its freedom. In addition, many members of Congress who were restive, were reluctant to express opposition in fear of embarrassing the president. Those who did criticize, expressed such diverse opinions that their influence on the president was slight.

Also in late February, the administration gave another indication that

IX. The Decision to Escalate

it might further escalate in Vietnam. A "white paper" was issued, giving a detailed, documented case charging North Vietnam with flagrant and increasing aggression against South Vietnam. The charge was accompanied by a warning that the United States might be compelled to escalate if the Communist aggression did not cease. The "white paper" appeared to have a twofold purpose: to provide a justification for continuing American airstrikes against targets in North Vietnam, and to reinforce the administration's position that any negotiations on the Vietnamese crisis were impossible until North Vietnam ceased its aggression. The document hinted at an increasing American military involvement and placed the responsibility on Hanoi.

The air war begun in February provided the pretext for the sending of U.S. ground troops to Vietnam. On March 7, the first ground troops (3,500 Marines) landed in South Vietnam. From the air war over the north to ground troops in the south, the mission had gone far beyond merely protecting air bases. By the end of March, 38,000 U.S. Marines were stationed in South Vietnam. Also at that time, the U.S. military requested an additional 40,000 troops.

Events in Vietnam and the issuance of the "white paper" started a new round of Senate debate in early March. Overall, the Johnson administration's policy continued to command broad support in the Senate. Senator William Proxmire said the administration policies were "the best chance for us to achieve that enduring peace in the enormously complex situation." Senators Gale McGee, Hugh Scott, and Howard Cannon also expressed their support of the administration. The strongest dissents predictably came from Morse and Gruening. Morse called the "white paper" a "rationalization" that might "best be described as a Swiss cheese." Gruening said the "white paper" added "no new facts to [clear] the already muddy water" of the Vietnam situation.[11]

In early April, the administration again escalated the American commitment in Vietnam, deciding upon the assignment of additional thousands of troops and continued American air strikes against North Vietnam. To pacify his critics in Congress and to gain greater public support, Johnson delivered his notable Johns Hopkins University speech on April 7, declaring that the United States was ready to begin, without prior conditions, diplomatic discussions to end the war. He also said he would ask Congress to approve a $1 billion American investment in a vast Southeast Asia regional development program that eventually could include North

Vietnam. This speech was the first statement of a willingness by the United States to enter negotiations on Vietnam without prior conditions. Heretofore, the administration had said that negotiations could begin only after some signal from North Vietnam that it was willing to end aggression against its southern neighbor.

Members of Congress differed widely in their reaction to President Johnson's speech, as they had in all his previous Vietnam policies. Democrats generally praised it as "moving and constructive," while many Republicans accused Johnson of trying to buy peace in Southeast Asia. The Senate Republican leader, Dirksen, sounded the keynote for his side of the aisle when he criticized the president's suggesting the $1 billion aid program to raise Southeast Asian living standards. "Do you buy freedom for a humble people with the billion dollar package? I doubt it and doubt also that we can preserve face and prestige with such an approach."[12] On the other hand, Senator Mansfield accepted the policy speech as a "profoundly moving and constructive statement which reveals both the strength of President Johnson's resolve and his deep concern for the welfare of all the people."[13] Other Democrats, however, tended to be more critical of the president's proposals. Once again, the diverse, confused reactions of the Senate probably indicated the president could continue his policies unhindered.

In the ensuing weeks, senatorial comments on the Vietnam quagmire continued to lack a general direction. On April 18, Fulbright urged a halt to the bombing of North Vietnam "to give their people a little time to contemplate the trouble." Two days later, Mansfield also urged a cease-fire and a bombing halt, simultaneously calling for a multination conference on Vietnam as "the last thin hope of peace these before events move beyond the reach of hope." On the other hand, Morse called for the removal of Secretary McNamara and Secretary Rusk. A leading "hawk," Senator Russell Long, hammered away in the other direction, stating that "modern-day appeasers and isolationists were undermining Mr. Johnson's policy in Vietnam [and leading] the Communists to believe that the United States would surrender all of Asia."[14]

The president was clearly watching the Senate's reaction to his Vietnam policy. Apparently, he was not interested in criticism or advice, but in approval and support. After almost every dissenting speech, except those by Morse and Gruening, Johnson sent an administration official to try to bring the critic around, with varying success. Twice he invited all

IX. The Decision to Escalate

(*Left to right*) Secretary of State Dean Rusk, President Lyndon Johnson, and Defense Secretary Robert McNamara, architects of the Vietnam policy (LBJ Presidential Library and Museum).

members of the Senate to the White House for detailed briefings on the war and his policy. President Johnson was reported to believe that much of the criticism represented the opinion of men without access to necessary information.

In early May 1965, President Johnson asked for and received a new endorsement from Congress for his Vietnam policies, almost as significant as the Tonkin Gulf Resolution, in the form of an additional $700 million appropriation to finance the war. Johnson had inserted in this resolution a passage wherein Congress clearly endorsed his Vietnam policy. In it, the president stressed that the bill was "not a routine appropriation Each member of Congress who supports the request is also voting to persist in our effort to halt Communist aggression in South Vietnam. Each is saying that the Congress and the president stand united before the world in joint determination that the independence of South Vietnam shall be preserved and the Communist attack will not succeed."[15]

Despite the reservations of individual senators, Senator Russell correctly prophesied: "He'll get all the money he has asked Congress for. While there may be some divergence of opinion, this has become a matter of national prestige so that even some of those who don't agree with the president's course will go forward."[16] Congress approved the resolution quickly and without dissent. Obviously, it was very difficult to vote against supporting soldiers in combat. Johnson said this vote and the Tonkin Gulf Resolution showed that Congress backed his policies.

In another move to disarm his critics and to solidify his support in Congress, Johnson ordered a bombing halt in May 1965. However, he refused to alter his basic policy—preserving an independent, non–Communist South Vietnam—and no compromise was reached with the Communists.

At this time, the war continued to worsen. The bombing as well as sending more troops and more aid had failed to turn the tide. At the end of May, General Westmoreland said that only large increases in U.S. forces could avert defeat. Making the situation even worse was the absence of a strong government in South Vietnam.

That month, Marshall Nguyan Cao Ky and General Nguyan Van Thieu emerged as the new leaders of the nation. This was the fifth government since the overthrow of Diem in November 1963. The U.S. government was not impressed with the new appointees, representing "the bottom of the barrel," one American official stated. Especially embarrassing was Marshall Ky's comment that Adolf Hitler was one of his heroes.[17]

In early June, there were indications of a continuing American escalation. On June 5, the State Department acknowledged publicly for the first time that American ground troops in South Vietnam were engaging in combat in defense of key installations against Communist guerrillas. Previously the department had insisted that American troops merely performed advisory and defensive roles and only returned fire in self-defense. The Defense Department acknowledged at least 42,000 American troops in South Vietnam; this was twice the number present in early March when the first Marines landed to protect the airbase at Danang. The public also learned that President Johnson had authorized his commanders in Vietnam to commit American ground forces to combat if assistance was requested by the South Vietnamese Army. Officials indicated that the expanded combat role would necessitate the assignment of additional American troops to South Vietnam.

This newly acknowledged role of the American forces led to a short-

IX. The Decision to Escalate

lived Senate debate on whether the United States was moving into an undeclared war on the Asian mainland. Senator Javits sparked the discussion with a statement, warning that "we have been moving in the direction of a massive, bogged down land struggle in Asia without any specific consent by Congress or the people for that kind of war." Javits proposed that the president ask Congress for a resolution specifically authorizing an expansion of the United States military role. Without such a congressional mandate, he said, "a United States land struggle in Asia could engender criticism and division in the country that will make recent protests look like a high school picnic."[18]

Senator Gruening responded by ruefully pointing to the Tonkin Gulf Resolution which "enables the president to take all necessary steps to assist South Vietnam defend its freedom." Senator McGee also stated that the president already possessed the necessary authorization for his policies. "Time won't afford us the semantic luxury of debate over the terms of declared war."[19]

To mollify his Senate critics, the president had Senator Fulbright deliver a speech emphasizing that the administration was committed to the goal of ending the war as soon as possible by negotiations without conditions. Fulbright suggested an end to the American escalation to be replaced by a "resolute but restrained" holding action in Vietnam until the Communists saw the futility of trying to win a complete military victory and agreed to negotiate. He was equally opposed to unconditional withdrawal of American forces or to escalation of the war. Unconditional withdrawal, he said, would have "disastrous consequences" extending beyond South Vietnam. It would "betray our obligation to a country we promised to defend, destroy the credibility of other American guarantees and encourage Peking to believe that guerrilla warfare was a relatively safe and inexpensive way of expanding Communist power."[20]

On the other hand, he added, it was also apparent that the forces of South Vietnam

Senator Jacob Javits, an early "hawk" who later opposed U.S. escalation in 1965 (U.S. Senate Historical Office).

and the United States could win a complete victory only "at a cost far exceeding the requirements of our interests and our honor." The United States should sustain the South Vietnamese Army "so as to persuade the Communists that Saigon could not be crushed and that the United States will not be driven from South Vietnam."[21] In delivering the speech, Fulbright acted on his belief that he could only influence President Johnson by supporting him publicly.

By this time, Vietnam was becoming even more of a partisan issue for the president. The liberal flank of the Democratic Party criticized him as too warlike and urged him to seek a negotiated solution. The more "hawkish" Republican leadership was reverting to the Goldwater objective of total victory over the Communists, with a new reliance on aerial bombardment of targets in the areas of Hanoi and Haiphong. Dirksen announced that Fulbright's speech had "raised doubt" among Republicans that the Vietnam policy of the administration was what they thought it to be. The Republicans would not stand for the admission of Communists in the government of South Vietnam, and "any [meaning Fulbright] who talk of concessions by the United States have an obligation to specify the kinds that are prepared to advocate and to indicate the limits beyond which concessions cannot made." These comments paved the way for a future withdrawal of Republican support should developments in the Vietnam war prove unfavorable. Despite this Republican pressure, however, the fundamental impetus for escalation continued to come from the White House.

In late June, amid rumors of another U.S. escalation, the Vietnam debate heated up again. This followed calls for further troop increases by General Taylor, then Chairman of the Joint Chiefs, and Secretary of Defense McNamara. The Senate debate was led by Church whose main purpose in speaking out after a four-month silence, was a strong feeling that "further escalation of the war northward should be resolutely resisted." He urged the administration to solicit some kind of United Nations involvement, to affirm more formally its willingness to deal with the Vietcong as part of any Communist delegation and to advocate "genuine self-determination" for the people of South Vietnam. He asked the administration not to confuse an exercise in power politics with the fight for freedom, contending that the regime in Saigon was as dictatorial as the one in Hanoi. Above all, Church urged a continued and full debate lest Congress become a "mock parliament."[22]

Senator Javits seconded Church's call for a wider Senate debate. In

IX. The Decision to Escalate

order to spur a full debate in both houses of Congress, he renewed his proposal that the legislators consider a new resolution regarding President Johnson's use of force and designating a cease-fire and negotiations as the objectives of policy.

Despite these periodic outbursts of "dovism," the Vietnam commitment spiraled upward. On July 27, the "Rubicon" was crossed when the president announced American military strength would be increased from 75,000 to 125,000 "almost immediately." He added that "more will be sent as needed. "Johnson's decision came in spite of dissenting appeals from a number of prominent senators, including Mansfield, Russell, Fulbright, Aiken, and Cooper. At a meeting of congressional leaders the night before Johnson made public his decision to escalate, Mansfield read a long statement expressing fears about the stability of the South Vietnamese government, the dangers of escalation, and the possibility of a damaging Senate debate. Johnson overruled Mansfield's concerns, and moved ahead with his escalation policy. The president, while holding to the sharp increase of troops, decided to postpone any calling up of the reserves in order to avoid such a debate.

In his July meetings with congressional leaders, Johnson promised the conservatives he would hold the line in Vietnam, and also promised the liberals he would not let the war get out of hand. These pledges enabled the president to maintain his support in Congress.

At the time of the July decision to escalate, the Senate was divided into roughly four groups: the extreme doves, such as Morse and Gruening; the hawks, such as Dirksen, Dodd, and Tower; the persistent but temperate doves, such as Fulbright, Kennedy (New York), Javits, and Aiken; and the silent majority, such as Russell.

The failure of the silent majority to speak out and voice opposition was certainly the key to senatorial acquiescence in Johnson's policy of escalation which reached a climax in July 1965. Several factors underlay their silence. There was extreme reluctance to create the impression of disunity while American servicemen were fighting abroad. They realized that Johnson inherited the Vietnam problem from his predecessors and had been plagued by the weakness of the Saigon regime as well as the unwillingness of the Communists to compromise. They had no alternative to offer, and would not advocate military withdrawal under fire. Furthermore, some feared that the charge of "appeasement of Communism" would be hurled at them should they challenge the president's position. The United States was now fully engaged in what would be a long and frustrating war, later to become the subject of much "finger-pointing" and regret.

The inconclusive debates in the Senate were noted by the press. The *Detroit Free Press* editorialized: "Time was when great debates on foreign policy enlivened the Senate and informed the nation. But today the voices of opposition are muted. We have today no Borahs, Tafts, or LaFollettes to challenge the creed of conformity. No men of great moral courage who would risk defeat rather than surrender a shred of principle. The voices of dissent have been stilled, and the great issues are smothered by a pall of mediocrity."[23]

The president's decision of July 27, marked the beginning of an American land war in Asia. Despite the occasional chorus of vocal dissent in the Senate and the obvious underlying reservations, President Johnson successfully imposed a fait accompli upon the Senate. Through its confused and diverse responses to the president's previous actions, the Senate had paved the way for each succeeding escalation until the president's crucial decision was announced on July 27, 1965. Years later, in the tragic aftermath of this decision, the Senate would belatedly assert more of its foreign policy initiative in an abortive attempt to correct this policy and placate public opinion. Nevertheless, the Vietnam problem would not disappear. As in nearly all the crises of the post–World War II era, the Senate had clearly played a secondary role in the final decision.

The tendency of the Senate to readily "consent" existed during the Eisenhower and Kennedy administrations also. Yet neither of these presidents took such a highhanded attitude toward the Senate regarding Vietnam as did President Johnson. Possibly the explanation lies in the different situations under which each president operated. The crisis in Vietnam had reached a critical level during the Johnson presidency. Another explanation relates to the varying political backgrounds of the three presidents. Eisenhower was not only politically inexperienced, but also did not believe in browbeating Congress, partly because of the Bricker Amendment controversy of the early 1950s. Kennedy, like Johnson, a former senator, had never been a Senate leader and had been elected by a very small majority. Johnson, as majority leader, had been the "boss" of the Senate, and had usually gotten his own way. Elected president by an overwhelming majority, he could continue to browbeat the Senate as he had done in the past. The Johnson method had proved spectacularly successful before 1960 and as president, he would continue this method again after 1963.

X

Conclusions

Early in 1966, Senator Richard Russell declared on the Senate floor during the consideration of supplementary authorization of funds for escalating the war in Vietnam: "I am a congressional man. I have stood here for more than 30 years and deplored—almost wept over—the slow erosion of congressional power that has placed this body in a position inferior to the other branches of the government. The whole genius of our government was to provide three coequal branches—legislative, executive, and judicial.[1] The Senate's extremely limited role in formulating the Vietnam policy is a clear example of this decline.

Through 1965, four presidents gradually escalated the United States' role in a vain attempt to settle the Vietnam problem. President Truman acted by bolstering French military power in the area. Eisenhower based his policy around the creation of an independent South Vietnam, presumably able to defend itself. Kennedy and Johnson substituted increasing amounts of American military power when the South Vietnamese proved unable to defend themselves. By 1965, the United States was at war in Asia over a problem few people really understood.

Ever since Truman announced the American intention to oppose the Vietnamese Communists in 1950, the Senate played a secondary role in shaping Vietnam policy. Very few senators ever demonstrated expertise or great interest in this problem. Most senators showed little concern over senatorial impotence in foreign policy. The dangerous situation was thereby created where the executive made the vital decisions regarding Vietnam, virtually unchecked by Congress. A strong-willed president might engage the United States in war over Vietnam, with the Senate helplessly shackled by its incompetence and lack of initiative.

The intriguing question remains why a problem which hovered on the international scene for decades attracted such limited interest or so little study until the mid–1960s. As late as 1965, the Senate's attitude toward Vietnam could be described as confused and undirected. The essential guidelines of American foreign policy—the containment policy and the domino theory—unchanged since the post–World War II period would therefore suffer a brutal test in the jungles of Vietnam.

Had the principles underlying the Cold War undergone a change since the Russo-American diplomatic challenges of the late 1940s? Was the United States truly an omnipotent, omniscient power? Could a Communist movement actually attract strong loyalty from the people of that country? Was it in the American interests to cover every "hole in the dike" that shielded the West from communism? Neither the president nor the Senate sufficiently considered these questions in the context of Southeast Asia. The Senate thus proved to be an acquiescent partner in the Vietnam policy.

During the 1950s and 1960s, the Senate would occasionally protest the executive's dominant role in foreign policy or the possibility of America getting involved too deeply in the Vietnam quagmire. Yet no Senate amendment to restrict the president's policy ever passed. Despite the occasional rhetoric, the president was given virtually carte blanche by a confused, but hopeful Senate. Senators never achieved unity on any Vietnam position through 1965, and their scattered opinions gave the president the freedom he needed to act.

How might future fait accomplis by the president be avoided? The Senate must perform its role as a watchdog of foreign policy more carefully. In particular, the Foreign Relations and Armed Services Committees must oversee more closely the president's handling of foreign policy. A closer cooperation between the president and Congress, particularly in the flow of information, is essential. The key to such cooperation lies with the president. Should he choose not to take Congress into his confidence, the trend toward executive "tyranny" over foreign policy will continue. Uninformed and unwilling to repudiate the president, the Senate would be forced into a secondary role perpetually.

Even with closer executive-congressional cooperation, the president will probably continue to dominate the handling of foreign policy. Writing in 1970, Senator Jacob Javits stated:

> Essentially, the constitutional role of the United States Senate in foreign policy is consultative. Our powers are not comparable to those of the presidency. The one weapon we have, the purse—must necessarily be used with the greatest discretion.

X. Conclusions

The use of such power in foreign policy through denying appropriations implies a rejection of the American president, almost as stunning as a vote of no-confidence under the parliamentary system which therefore ousts the government. It could, in all probability, make it very difficult thereafter for the president to perform the executive function in foreign policy areas having little or nothing to do with the case in point.[2]

Senator Javits' article thereby leads to the somber, disturbing question: Could another "Vietnam," without the consent or thorough understanding of the Senate, happen again?

Chapter Notes

Chapter I

1. Alexis de Tocqueville, *Democracy in America* (New York: G. Adland, 1938), 215.
2. Wilfred Binkley, *President and Congress* (New York: Vintage, 1962), 8.
3. *Congressional Digest* XXVIII (June–July 1945), 165.
4. *Ibid.*, 166.
5. Edward Corwin, *The President, Office and Powers, 1781–1957* (New York: New York University Press, 1957), 171.
6. William Maclay, *The Journal of William Maclay: United States Senator from Pennsylvania, 1789–1791* (New York: A. & C. Boni, 1927), 128.
7. Arthur Schlesinger and Alfred DeGrazia, *Congress and the Presidency* (Washington, D.C.: American Enterprise Institute for Public Policy Research, 1967), 20.
8. J. D. Richardson, *Compilation of the Messages and Papers of the Presidents, 1789–1902*, 11 vols. (New York: Bureau of National Literature and Art, 1925), I, 314–15.
9. Thomas Bailey, *A Diplomatic History of the American People*, 7th ed. (New York: Appleton-Century-Crofts, 1964), 257.
10. Richardson, *Compilation*, IV, 442.
11. *Abridgement of the Debates in Congress from 1789 to 1865*, 16 vols., 29th Congress, 1st session (New York: D. Appleton, 1856), IV, 303.
12. John G. Nicolay and John Hay, *Complete Works of Abraham Lincoln*, 10 vols. (New York: Lamb, 1894), X, 1.
13. Clinton Rossiter, *The American Presidency* (New York: Harcourt Brace, 1960), 111–12.
14. Binkley, *President*, 248.
15. Schlesinger and DeGrazia, *Congress*, 25–26.
16. Theodore Roosevelt, *Autobiography* (New York: Charles Scribner's Sons, 1914), 389.
17. Rossiter, *Presidency*, 85.
18. *Congressional Digest* XXVIII (June–July 1949), 181.
19. Austin, Anthony, *The President's War* (Philadelphia: J. P. Lippincott, 1971), 2.
20. *Ibid.*, 3.
21. E. W. Kenworthy, "Fulbright Becomes a National Issue," *New York Times*, October 1, 1961, 263.
22. Kenneth Grundy, "The Apprenticeship of J. William Fulbright," *Virginia Quarterly Review* XLIII (Summer 1967), 383.

Chapter II

1. *New York Times*, March 31, 1945, 13.
2. Robert Scheer, "How the United States Got Involved in Vietnam," Center for the Study of Democratic Institutions, Santa Barbara, 1967, 4.
3. William Bullitt, "The Saddest War," *Life* XXIII (December 29, 1947), 64–66.
4. *Congressional Record*, 80th Congress, 2nd session, 7620.
5. David Schoenbrum, *Vietnam: How We Got In, How We Get Out* (New York: Atheneum, 1968), 26–27.

6. George Herring, *America's Longest War: The United States and Vietnam, 1950–1975* (New York: McGraw-Hill, 1996), 20.
7. Norman Graebner, *The New Isolationism* (New York: Ronald Press, 1956), 3.
8. *Ibid.*, 14.
9. *Ibid.*, 16–17.
10. *Congressional Digest* XXX (1951), 44.
11. *Ibid.*, 52.
12. *Ibid.*, 58.
13. *Ibid.*, 27.
14. Herring, *America's Longest War*, 20.
15. *New York Times*, May 14, 1950.
16. *Ibid.*, 21.
17. *Congrssional Record*, 80th Congress, 2nd session, 17000.
18. *Ibid.*, 17000.
19. *Ibid.*, 81st Congress, 1st session, 10756.
20. *Ibid.*, 81st Congress, 2nd session, 170.
21. *Ibid.*
22. *New York Times*, May 4, 1953, 6.
23. *Congressional Record*, 83rd Congress, 1st session, 7638.
24. *Ibid.*, 7639.
25. *Ibid.*, 7635.
26. *Ibid.*
27. *Ibid.*, 7623.
28. *Ibid.*
29. *Ibid.*, 7863.
30. *Ibid.*, 7610.
31. *Ibid.*
32. *Ibid.*, 10234.
33. Emmett Hughes, *The Ordeal of Power* (New York: Atheneum, 1963), 1444.
34. *Ibid.*, 145.
35. Binkley, *President and Congress*, 354.
36. Hughes, *Ordeal*, 124.
37. *Ibid.*
38. Binkley, *President and Congress*, 360–62.

Chapter III

1. *New York Times*, February 11, 1954, 1.
2. *Congressional Record*, 83rd Congress, 2nd session, 2903.
3. *New York Times*, March 20, 1954, 1.
4. *Ibid.*, March 28, 1954, 17.
5. *Ibid.*, March 30, 1954. 1.
6. *Congressional Record*, 83rd Congress, 2nd session, 4208.
7. *New York Times*, March 31, 1954, 1.
8. *Congressional Record*, 83rd Congress, 2nd session, 4673.
9. *New York Times*, April 11, 1954, 1.
10. *Ibid.*
11. *Ibid.*, April 17, 1954, 1.
12. Richard Nixon, *No More Vietnams* (New York: Arbor House, 1985), 30.
13. *New York Times*, April 27, 1954.
14. Alan Axelrod, *The Real History of the Vietnam War* (Toronto: Sterling, 2013), 65.
15. *New York Times*, May 29, 194, 3.
16. Chalmers Roberts, "The Day We Didn't Go to War," *Reporter* XI (September 14, 1954), 35.
17. *New York Times*, April 25, 1954, IV, 3.
18. Dwight Eisenhower, *Mandate For Change* (Garden City, NY: Doubleday, 1962), 11.
19. Matthew Ridgeway, *Soldier* (New York: Harper, 1956), 257.
20. Melvin Gurtov, *The First Vietnam War* (New York: Columbia University Press, 1967), 136.
21. *New York Times*, May 23, 1954, IV, 10.
22. *Public Papers of the Presidents of the United States* (Washington, D.C.: Government Printing Office, 1960), Dwight D. Eisenhower, 1954, 366.
23. Sherman Adams, *First-Hand Report* (New York: Harper, 1961), 121.

Chapter IV

1. *Congressional Record*, 83rd Congress, 2nd session, 10139.
2. *Department of State Bulletin* XXX, no. 772, April 12, 1954 (Washington, D.C.: Government Printing Office, 1954), 540.
3. *New York Times*, March 31, 1954, 1.
4. Eisenhower, *Mandate*, 347.
5. *Ibid.*, 346–47.
6. *New York Times*, April 9, 1954, 1.

7. Anthony Eden, *Full Circle* (Boston: Houghton Mifflin, 1960), 104.
8. *New York Times*, April 18, 1954, 1.
9. *Ibid.*, April 2, 1954, 4.
10. Cited in *Congressional Record*, 83rd Congress, 2nd session, 7921.
11. *New York Times*, May 6, 1954, 19.
12. *Ibid.*
13. *Ibid.*, May 11, 1954, 1.
14. *Ibid.*, May 9, 1954, IV, 10.
15. *Ibid.*, May 21, 1954, 1.
16. Charles Lerche, "The United States, Great Britain, and SEATO: A Case Study in the Fait Accompli," *Journal of Politics* XVIII (August 1956), 459–79.
17. *Congressional Record*, 83rd Congress, 2nd session, 3721–23.
18. *New York Times*, July 1, 1954, 1.
19. Taylor Parks, et al., *American Foreign Policy, 1950–1955*, Department of State Publication 6446, General Foreign Policy Series 117 (Washington, D.C.: Government Printing Office, 1957), 941.
20. U.S. Congress, Senate Committee on Foreign Relations, *The Southeast Asia Collective Defense Treaty*, Hearings Before the Subcommittee of the Committee on Foreign Relations, 83rd Congress, 2nd session, November 11, 1954, I, 21.
21. *Ibid.*, 84th Congress, 1st session, January 10, 1955, II, 47.
22. cited in Parks, et al., *American Foreign Policy 1950–1955*, 47.
23. Hearings Before the Subcommittee of the Committee on Foreign Relations, 83rd Congress, 2nd session, I, 25.
24. *Ibid.*
25. Hans Morganthau, "Military Illusions," *New Republic* CXXXIV (March 19, 1956), 16.

Chapter V

1. *New York Times*, February 20, 1954.
2. *Ibid.*, February 23, 1954, 1.
3. *Ibid.*
4. *Ibid.*, March 28, 1954, IV, E3.
5. *Congressional Record*, 83rd Congress, 2nd session, A3307.
6. *New York Times*, April 28, 1954, IV, 3.
7. "The Issues at Geneva," press release no. 238, series S, no. 15, May 7, 1954 (Washington, D.C.: Department of State, Public Service Division, 1954), 9–10.
8. *Congressional Record*, 83rd Congress, 2nd session, 6268–71.
9. *Ibid.*, 6245.
10. *New York Times*, May 26, 1954, 2.
11. John Foster Dulles, "Security in the Pacific," press release no. 318, series S, no. 20 (Washington, D.C.: Department of State Bulletin, Public Services Division, 1954), XXX, no. 783 (June 28, 194), 73.
12. *Congressional Record*, 83rd Congress, 2nd session, 8343.
13. *New York Times*, July 2, 1954, 2.
14. *Congressional Record*, 83rd Congress, 2nd session, 9045.
15. *Ibid.*, 9947–10011.
16. *Ibid.*, 9997–10010.
17. *Ibid.*, 10135.
18. *New York Times*, July 17, 1954, 2.
19. *Ibid.*, July 18, 1954, IV, 1.
20. Herring, *America's Longest War*, 43.
21. John R. Beal, *John Foster Dulles* (New York: Harper, 1957), 212–14.
22. Anthony Eden, *Full Circle* (Boston: Houghton Mifflin, 1960), 139.
23. Selig Harrison, "Kennedy as President," *New Republic* CXLII (June 27, 1960), 15.
24. Selig Harrison, "Poker Playing Stu," *New Republic* CXLII (June 20, 1960), 12.
25. *New York Times*, July 25, 1954, 5.

Chapter VI

1. Herring, *America's Longest War*, 53.
2. Robert Scheer and Walter Hinkle, "The Vietnam Lobby," in the *Vietnam Reader*, ed. Bernard Fall and Marcus Raskin (New York: Random House, 1965), 80.
3. U.S. Congress, Senate Committee on Foreign Relations, Report on Indochina, 83rd Congress, 2nd session, 1954, 11.
4. *Department of State Bulletin* XXXI, no. 803 (November 15, 1954), 735–36.
5. Kahin and Lewis, *The United States in Vietnam*, 68.
6. *Ibid.*, 71.
7. *Ibid.*
8. Graebner, *Isolationism*, 202–03.
9. *New York Times*, July 21, 1955, 22.

10. Williams, et al., *America in Vietnam*, 140.
11. U.S. Congress, Senate Committee on Foreign Relations, Report on Indochina, 84th Congress, 1st session, 1955, 13–14.
12. *Congressional Record*, 84th Congress, 1st session, 6104.
13. *Department of State Bulletin* XXXIV, no. 885 (June 11, 1956), 972–74.
14. Mike Mansfield, " Reprieve in Vietnam," *Harpers* CCXII (January 1956), 46–51.
15. John F. Kennedy, "America's Stake in Vietnam," *Vital Speeches* XXII (April 1, 1956), 617–19.
16. *Ibid.*
17. *Ibid.*
18. Mike Mansfield, "Watch All Trouble Areas, Not Just Mideast," *U.S. News and World Report* XXII (February 8, 1957), 118–20.
19. *Ibid.*
20. Herring, *America's Longest War*, 54.
21. *Congressional Record*, 85th Congress, 1st session, 6259, 6254.
22. *Congressional Record*, 85th Congress, 1st session, 6759–64.
23. *New York Times*, May 12, 1957, IV, 7.
24. *Congressional Record*, 85th Congress, 2nd session, 9467.
25. *Ibid.*
26. David Turner, *Mike Mansfield and Vietnam* (unpublished doctoral dissertation, University of Kentucky, 1984), 104.
27. *New York Times*, December 16, 1959, 17; December 18, 1959, 11.
28. *Ibid.*, February 9, 1960, 3.
29. *Congressional Record*, 90th Congress, 1st session, 27992.
30. *Ibid.*, 86th Congress, 1st session, 12773–77.

Chapter VII

1. Neil Sheehan, et al., eds., *Pentagon Papers* (New York: Bantam Press, 1971), 108.
2. *New York Times*, May 6, 1961, 3.
3. *Congressional Record*, 87th Congress, 1st session, 11702–25.
4. *Ibid.*, 9178.
5. *New York Times*, October 12, 1961.
6. Schlesinger, *A Thousand Days*, 547.
7. *New York Time*, February 16, 1962, 1, 6.
8. *Congressional Record*, 87th Congress, 2nd session, 2362.
9. *Ibid.*, 3861.
10. *Ibid.*, 8770.
11. *Ibid.*, 10048, 10050.
12. *Ibid.*, 14696.
13. *Department of State Bulletin* XLVIII, no. 1232 (February 4, 1962), 159; Schlesinger, *A Thousand Days*, 759.
14. Joseph Buttinger, *Vietnam: A Political History* (New York: Praeger, 1968), 461.
15. U.S. Congress, Senate Committee on Foreign Relations, Vietnam and Southeast Asia, Report of Senator Mike Mansfield, Senator J. Caleb Buggs, Senator Claiborne Pell, and Senator Benjamin Smith, 88th Congress, 1st session, 111.
16. *Ibid.*, 8–9.
17. *Congressional Record*, 88th Congress, 1st session, 9442.
18. *Ibid.*, 7309.
19. Herring, *America's Longest War*, 108.
20. *New York Times*, July 7, 1963, IV, 5.
21. *Public Papers, Kennedy*, 1963, 652.
22. *New York Times*, September 10, 1963, 1.
23. Herring, *America's Longest War*, 83.
24. *Public Papers, Kennedy*, 1963, 659–60.
25. *Congressional Record*, 88th Congress, 1st session, 18205.
26. *Ibid.*, 16824.
27. *Ibid.*, 17596.
28. *New York Times*, July 25, 1962, 4.
29. Sheehan, et al., *Pentagon Papers*, 166.
30. *New York Times*, November 2, 1963, 2.
31. *Ibid.*
32. John Dallas Stempel, "Policy Decision Making in the Department of State: The Vietnamese Problem, 1961–1965" (unpublished doctoral dissertation, University of California, Berkeley, 1965), 200.
33. Schlesinger, *A Thousand Days*, 997.
34. Kenneth O'Donnell, "LBJ and the Kennedys," *Life* LXIX (August 7, 1970),

51–52; *New York Times*, August 3, 1970, 16.
35. Roger Hilsman, *To Move a Nation* (Garden City, NY: Doubleday, 1967), 22–23; Sheehan, et al., *Pentagon Papers*, 81, 199.
36. Sorenson, *Kennedy*, 653.
37. Sheehan, et al., *Pentagon Papers*, 107.

Chapter VIII

1. Tom Wicker, *JFK and LBJ* (New York: William Morrow, 1968), 244.
2. Eric Goldman, *The Tragedy of Lyndon Johnson* (New York: Knopf, 1968), 379–82.
3. *Congressional Record*, 88th Congress, 2nd session, A1193.
4. *New York Times*, February 21, 1964, 16.
5. *Congressional Record*, 88th Congress, 2nd session, 3277–81.
6. *Ibid.*, 4780–82.
7. *New York Times*, March 21, 1964, 2.
8. *Ibid.*, March 2, 1964, IV, 9.
9. *Congressional Record*, 88th Congress, 2nd session, 4986–92.
10. *New York Times*, March 21, 1964, 2.
11. *Congressional Record*, 88th Congress, 2nd session, 6232.
12. *Ibid.*
13. *Ibid.*
14. *New York Times*, March 27, 1964, 1, 9.
15. Sheehan, *Pentagon Papers*, 235.
16. *Congressional Record*, 88th Congress, 2nd session, 6575–78.
17. *New York Times*, April 25, 1964, 2.
18. *Congressional Record*, 88th Congress, 2nd session, 8324.
19. *Ibid.*, 8438–40.
20. *Ibid.*
21. *New York Times*, May 16, 1964, 1.
22. *Congressional Record*, 88th Congress, 2nd session, 11214.
23. *Ibid.*, 15787–90.
24. *Ibid.*, 12373.
25. Anthony Austin, *The President's War* (Philadelphia: J. B. Lippincott), 16.
26. *Ibid.*
27. *Congressional Record*, 88th Congress, 2nd session, 18447–48.
28. *Ibid.*, 18409–10.
29. *Ibid.*, 18410–11.
30. *Ibid.*, 18413.
31. *Ibid.*, 18443, 18446.
32. *Ibid.*, 18403.
33. *Ibid.*, 18459.
34. Joseph Goulden, *Truth Is the First Casualty* (New York: Rand McNally, 1969), 49.
35. Gruening and Beaser, *Vietnam Folly*, 326.
36. Private interview with Dean Rusk, University of Georgia, September 14, 1971.

Chapter IX

1. Rusk stated that this accounted for the diminution of senatorial criticism at this time. Rusk interview, September 14, 1971.
2. David Turner, *Mike Mansfield and Vietnam* (unpublished doctoral dissertation, University of Kentucky, 1984), 163.
3. "Interview with Senator Church," *Ramparts* 3, no. 5 (January 1965), 17–22.
4. *New York Times*, January 3, 1965.
5. *Ibid.*, January 7, 1965, 2.
6. *Ibid.*
7. Joseph Buttinger, *Vietnam: A Political History* (New York: Praeger, 1968), 484.
8. *New York Times*, February 18, 1965, 10.
9. *Congressional Record*, 89th Congress, 1st session, 3146.
10. *New York Times*, February 25, 1965.
11. *Congressional Record*, 89th Congress, 1st session, 3712.
12. *New York Times*, April 8, 1965, 17.
13. *Ibid.*
14. *Ibid.*, April 27, 1965, 10.
15. U.S. Congress, H. R. 157, A Request for an Additional Appropriation to Meet Mounting Military Requirements in Vietnam, 89th Congress, 1st session, 1.
16. *New York Times*, May 6, 1965, 16.
17. Schoenbrum, *Vietnam*, 108.

18. *Congressional Record*, 89th Congress, 1st session, 12983.
19. *Ibid.*, 12985.
20. *Ibid.*, 13656.
21. *Ibid.*, 13657.
22. *Ibid.*, 14103–07.
23. *Detroit Free Press*, April 4, 1965.

Chapter X

1. *Congressional Record*, 89 Congress, 2nd session, 4192.
2. Jacob Javits, "The Congressional Presence in Foreign Affairs," *Foreign Affairs* XLVIII, no. 2 (January 1970), 233–34.

Bibliography

General

Adams, Henry. "The Session." *North American Review* CXI (July 1870), 29–62.
Adams, Sherman. *First-Hand Report*. New York: Harper, 1961.
Austin, Antlhony. *The President's War*. Philadelphia: J. B. Lippincott, 1971.
Axelrod, Alan. *The Real History of the Vietnam War*. New York: Sterling, 1975.
Bailey, Thomas. *A Diplomatic History of the American People*, 7th ed. New York: Appleton-Century-Crofts, 1964.
Barck, Oscar. *A History of the United States Since 1945*. New York: Dell,1965.
Beal, John. *John Foster Dulles*. New York: Harper, 1957.
Binkley, Wilfred. *President and Congress*. New York: Vintage, 1962.
Bullitt, William. "The Saddest War." *Life* XXIII (December 29, 1947), 64–69.
Buttinger, Joseph. *Vietnam: A Political History*. New York: Praeger, 1968.
Corwin, Edward. *The President, Office and Powers, 1787–1957*, 3d rev. ed. New York: New York University Press, 1957.
de Tocqueville, Alexis. *Democracy in America*. New York: G. Adler, 1838.
Diem, Bui. *The Jaws of History*. Boston: Houghton Mifflin, 1987.
Dietz. *Republicans and Vietnam*.
Dulles, John Foster. "Policy for Security and Peace." *Foreign Affairs* XXXII (April 1954), 353–64.
_____. *War or Peace*. New York: Macmillan, 1950.
Farnsworth, David. *The Senate Committee on Foreign Relations*. Urbana: University of Illinois Press, 1961.
Fulbright, J. William. *The Arrogance of Power*. New York: Vintage, 1966.
Galloway, John. *The Gulf of Tonkin Resolution*. Rutherford, NJ: Fairleigh Dickinson University Press,1970.
Geyelin, Philip. *Lyndon B. Johnson and the World*. New York: Praeger, 1966.
Goldman, Eric. *The Tragedy of Lyndon Johnson*. New York: Knopf, 1960.
Goulden, Joseph. *Truth Is the First Casualty*. New York: Rand McNally, 1969.
Graebner, Norman. *The New Isolationism*. New York: Ronald Press, 1956.
Gruening, Ernest, and Alfred Beaser. *Vietnam Folly*. Washington, D.C.: National Press, 1968.
Grundy, Kenneth. "The Apprenticeship of J. William Fulbright." *Quarterly Review Virginia* XLIII (Summer 1967), 82–99.
Gurtov, Melvin. *The First Vietnam Crisis*. New York: Columbia University Press, 1967.
Harrison, Selig. "Kennedy as President." *New Republic* CXLII (June 27, 1960), 9–15.
_____. "Lyndon Johnson's World." *New Republic* CXLII (June 13, 1960), 15–23.
_____. "Poker Playing Stu." *New Republic* CXLII (June 20, 1960), 11–16.

Bibliography

Herring, George. *America's Longest War*. New York: McGraw-Hill, 1996.
Hilsman, Roger. "Congressional-Executive Relations and the Foreign Policy Consensus." *American Political Science Review* LII (September 1958), 725–44.
_____. *To Move a Nation*. Garden City, NY: Doubleday, 1967.
Hughes, Emmet. *The Ordeal of Power*. New York: Atheneum, 1963.
"Interview with Senator Church," *Ramparts* 3, no. 5 (January 1965), 17–22.
Javits, Jacob. "The Congressional Presences in Foreign Affairs." *Foreign Affairs* XLVIII, no. 2 (January 1970), 233–34.
Jewell, Malcolm. *Senatorial Politics and Foreign Policy*. Lexington: University of Kentucky Press, 1962.
Johnson, Haynes, and Bernard Gwertzman. *Fulbright the Dissenter*. Garden City, NY: Doubleday, 1968.
Johnson, Lyndon. "Positive Steps in Foreign Policy." *Vital Speeches* XXV (June 1959), 502–04.
Kahin, George, and John Lewis. *The United States in Vietnam*. New York: Dial Press, 1967.
Kennedy, John F. "America's Stake in Vietnam." *Vital Speeches* XXII (August 1956), 617–23.
Kenworthy, E. W. "Fulbright Becomes a National Issue." *York New Times*, October 1, 1961, 21, 89–91.
Koenig, Louis. *The Chief Executive*. New York: Harcourt, Brace and World, 1968.
Kolodziej, Edward A. "Congress and Foreign Policy: Through the Looking Glass." *Virginia Quarterly Review* XLII (Winter 1966), 21.
_____. "Congress and Foreign Policy: The Timid Political Will." *Nation* CCII (March 14, 1966), 292–94.
LaFeber, Walter. *The New Empire*. Ithaca: Cornell University Press, 1963.
Lerche, Charles. "The United Statses, Geat Britain, and SEATO: A Case Study in the Fait Accompli." *Journal of Politics* XVIII (August 1956), 459–79.
Mansfield, Mike. "Reprieve in Vietnam." *Harpers* CCXII (January 1956), 46–51.
_____. "Watch All Trouble Areas, Not Just Mid-East." *U.S. News and World Report* XLII (February 8, 1957), 118–21.
Meyer, Karl. "Mr. Fulbright's Heresy." *New Statesman* LXVII (April 3, 1964), 512.
Morganthau, Hans. "Military Illusions." *New Republic* CXXXIV (March 11, 1956), 14–16.
Nixon, Richard. *No More Vietnams*. New York: Arbor House, 1985.
O'Donnell, Kenneth. "LBJ and the Kennedys." *Life* LXIX (August 7, 1970), 45–56.
Randle, Robert. *Geneva: 1954*. Princeton: Princeton University Press, 1969.
Roberts, Chalmers. "The Day We Didn't Go to War." *Reporter* XI (September 14, 1954) 31–35.
Rossiter, Clinton. *The American Presidency*. New York: Harcourt, Brace, 1960.
Scheer, Robert. *How the United States Got Involved in Vietnam*. Santa Barbara: Center for the Study of Democratic Institutions, 1965.
_____, and Walter Hinckle. "The Vietnam Lobby." *The Vietnam Reader*. Edited by Bernard Fall and Martin Raskin. New York: Random House, 1965.
Schlesinger, Arthur, Jr. *A Thousand Days*. Boston: Houghton Mifflin, 1965.
_____, and Alfred DeGrasia. *Congress and the Presidency*. Washington, D.C.: American Enterprise Institute for Public Policy Research, 1967.
Sheehan, Neil, et al., eds. *Pentagon Papers*. New York: Bantam, 1971.
Sorenson, Theodore. *Kennedy*. New York: Harper and Row, 1965.
Stempel, John Dallas. *Policy Decision Making in the Department of State: The Vietnamese Problem, 1961–1965*. Unpublished PhD dissertation, University of California, Berkeley, 1965.

Bibliography

Taylor, Maxwell. *Sword and Plowshares.* New York: Da Capo, 1972.
Thomas, M. Ladd. "A Critical Appraisal of SEATO." *Western Political Quarterly* X (December 1957), 926-36.
Turner, David M. *Mike Mansfield and Vietnam.* Unpublished doctoral dissertation, University of Kentucky, 1985.
"What Ridgeway Told Ike—War in Indochina Would Be Tougher Than Korea." *U.S. News and World Report* XXXVI (June 25, 1954), 30-32.
Wicker, Tom. *JFK and LBJ.* New York: William Morrow, 1968.
Williams, William A., et al., eds. *America in Vietnam.* Garden City, NY: Anchor Press, 1985.
Yarmolinsky, Adam. "American Foreign Policy and the Decision to Intervene." *Journal of International Affairs* XXII, no. 2 (1968), 231-35.

Memoirs

Eden, Anthony. *Full Circle.* Boston: Houghton Mifflin, 1960.
Eisenhower, Dwight. *Mandate for Change.* Garden City, NY: Doubleday, 1963.
Hull, Cordell. *Memoirs.* New York: Macmillan, 1948.
Maclay, William. *The Journal of William Maclay: United States Senator From Pennsylvania, 1789-1791.* New York: A. & C. Boni, 1927.
Ridgeway, Matthew. *Soldier.* New York: Harper, 1956.
Roosevelt, Theodore. *Autobiography.* New York: Charles Scribner's Sons, 1914.

Newspapers

Atlanta Constitution, May 3, 1970.
Christian Science Monitor, May 11, 1957.
New York Herald Tribune, May 13, 1957.
New York Times, 1945-1965.
Washington Post, May 13, 1957.

Other Sources

Lakeland, Peter. Private interview. Senator Jacob Javits' office, Washington, D.C., March 6, 1972.
McGovern, George. Personal letter, February 18, 1972.
Rusk, Dean. Private interview. University of Georgia, Athens, September 14, 1971.

Index

Numbers in *bold italics* indicate pages with illustrations

Acheson, Sec. of State Dean 20, *21*, 22
Adams, Pres. Sherman 5, 43, 136*n*23
advocates 19, 25, 52, 85, 92, 94, 95, 122, 128
Afghanistan 2
Africa 71, 83
aid appropriation 26, 27, 48, 107, 125, 133, 139*n*15
Aiken, Sen. George 97, 108, 111, 120, 129
Air Force: reduction 64; technicians 32–34, 39
airstrikes 118, 121, 123
alliance, SEATO 54; *see also* Southeast Asia Treaty Organization
allies 23, 36, 38, 46, 48, 50, 60–61, 83, 86, 103; Associated States 47, 62; British and other Western 43; Communist Chinese 61; European 37; U.S. French partnership 69
Allott, Sen. Gordon 90
ambassadors 3, 20, 74
American Southeast Asia policy 38, 78, 84
anti-communism 71, 73, 77
Ap Bac, battle of 91
Appropriations Committee 38; *see also* Bridges, Styles
Argentina 6
armed forces 4, 56
Armed Services Committee 36, 115, 132
armistice agreement 53, 62, 63, 68, 69
Army and Navy intelligence groups 11
Articles of Confederation 3
Asia 19, 24, 26, 27, 54, 62, 65, 71 83, 84, 86, 98, 106–108, 120, 124, 127, 131; aid to 91, 123–124; alliance to save 51, 83, 85; American land war in 106, 113, 130; communism in 28, 60, 65, 80, 85; Communist aggression in 28, 41, 48, 62, 80, 83, 90; defense pact 48, 51, 52, 53, 67, 70, 103, 114; democracy in 78; forces of change in 79, 127–128; free nations of 49; military assistance to 24, 37, 52, 84, 85, 113; Southeast Asia resolution 111; three divided lands in 81; troop commitments in 19, 22, 25, 37, 85, 98–99; U.S. policies in 18, 21, 23, 28, 38, 60, 77, 91, 96, 107; withdrawal of all American forces 34, 39; *see also* Southeast Asia Treaty Organization (SEATO)
Asian Munich 62
Associated States: independence 38; people of 26, 35
Austin, Anthony (historian) 109
Australia 54; *see also* SEATO alliance
Australia, New Zealand, and United States Security Pact (ANZUS) 45, 47, 51

Bailey, Thomas 7
Bartlett, Ruhl 12
Battle Line 88–89; *see also* Republican National Committee
Bayh, Sen. Birch 95
Beal, John R. 68
Belgium 53
Berlin 85, 88
Berlin conference 58–59
Bible, Sen. Allen 111
Bidault, George 59

145

Index

big four powers 58; *see also* Britain; France; Geneva Conference; Russia; United States
Bigart, Homer 96
Binkley, Wilfred 30
Boggs, Haley 91
Bolivar, Simon 6
Brewster, Sen. Owen 113
Bricker amendment 28–29, 130
Bridges, Styles 38, 59
Britain 48–49, 50, 51, 52, 62, 63, 67
British Commonwealth 47
British Crown 12
British Foreign Secretary 52, 67, 68; *see also* Eden, Anthony
British government 5, 31, 39, 48, 52, 68
British West Indies 5
Buddhists 14, 97; persecution of 95; raids 93
Buggs, Sen. J. Caleb 138n15
Bullitt, William 16
Burma 19, 52, 78
Bush, Sen. George W. 12
Butler, Hugh 23, 24
Byrd, Sen. Harry 120

Cabinet officers 8–9
Calhoun, John C. 7
Cambodia 22, 25, 26, 41, 50, 54, 62, 64, 68, 78, 102
campaign, presidential 24, 30, 85, 103, 117
Can, Ngo Dinh 77; *see also* Diem, Ngo
Canada 68
Cannon, Sen. Howard 123
Capitol Hill 34, 35
Carlson, Sen. Frank 95
Cass, Lewis 7
casualties of war 17, 18, 23, 40, 89, 103, 109, 117
cease-fire agreements 81
Celler, Emmanuel 73
Central Intelligence Agency 11
Ceylon 52
Chase-Smith, Sen. Margaret 104
chief executive 10, 29, 39
China 2, 15, 48, 69, 76, 79, 81, 94, 100, 106, 117; allies warning to 47; Communist China 18, 26, 34, 40, 43, 58–59, 61, 64, 68, 76, 77, 102, 107; communist victory in 20; fall of 16, 118; republics of 49; Vietminh delegation 69

Chinese foreign minister 69; *see also* En-lai, Chou
Christian Science Monitor 80
Church, Sen. Frank 95–96, 108, 118, 122, 139n3
Churchill, British Prime Minister Winston 15, 39, 47, 50, 53, 65
Civil War 8, 10
civilians 42
Cleveland, Grover 9
coalition, allied 37, 39, 43, 47–48, 63
Cold War 14, 15–16, 17–18, 20, 71, 73, 132; struggles of the 78, 82, 83
Collins, Gen. J. Lawton 74
colonial wars 98
colonialism 15, 22, 38, 85
Columbia, crisis with 10
commander-in-chief 4, 18, 113, 120; power of the president as 56
commerce, regulate foreign 4
communiqué, 48, 65, 67; Anglo-American 53
communism 20, 26, 38, 49, 60, 65, 78, 85, 94, 107–108, 129, 132
Communist movement 16, 82; Bien Hoa 118; Chinese 27, 46, 119; French 32; Indochina 35, 51, 64; North Vietnam 70; South Vietnam 91, 100, 101, 120–121, 123, 126, 127–128; Southeast Asia 41, 90–91. 99; Soviets 64; Vietnamese 32, 68, 92, 131
concessions, political 26, 67
conflicts with other nations 9, 12, 14, 36, 40
Congress: 3, 28–30, 33, 35, 39, 48–49, 59, 63, 84, 86, 94, 106, 122, 124; bipartisan congressional hearing 62; consulting with 54–56, 89, 106, 123, 127, 132; Democratic victory 76; endorsement from 125–26; joint resolution 36, **110**, 112; objections to American intervention in Vietnam 46, 58, 65, 108–109; requirement of a declaration of war by 34–35, 56, 111; Republican-dominated 76; support of a Pacific pact 51
Congress, the Spineless Branch 116; *see also* Gruening, Sen. Ernest
Congress, war-making power of 7, 12, 55
congressional: authorization 12, 19, 30, 34–36, 41–42, 46–47, 55, 58, 108, 120, 121–22, 127; relations 97, 129, 132

146

Index

Congressional Record 34
Connelly, Tom 23
Constitution 3, 56, 106; framers 12; preservation 8, 29; provision of advice and consent 4, 23–24
Constitutional Convention 4, 12
Constitutional fathers 4
Continental Congress 3
Cooper, Sen. John Sherman 37, 108, 129
Corwin, Edward 4
critics: 22–24, 26, 32–34, 41, 58, 64, 89, 97; of France's military efforts 38; of the Geneva Conference 60–61; of the Indochina crisis 25, 32–33, 39, 63, 65, 69; of U.S. involvement in Vietnam 23, 26, 62, 86, 90, 91, 104, 112, 119, 123, 124–126; of the war in Korea 30
Cuba 2, 9, 84–85, 89, 97; Bay of Pigs in 85, 97, 98; crisis of 1962 112
Czechoslovakia 58

Dai, Bao Vietnamese emperor 73, 74–75, 76
debate and action, ground rules for 11
debates 7, 18, 19, 23; congressional 29, 76, 113; constitutional war-making powers 55–56; cutting aid to Saigon 94; intervention 36–38; over French colonialism 16, 25; over the president's war-making initiative 35; over the Vietnam issue 89, 91, 98–99, 102, 106–107, 120, 128; over the war in Indochina 31–32, 34, 36; Senate 37–39, 55, 105, 115, 123, 127–130
declaration of war, congressional 12
Defense Secretary, *87*, 90, 96, 101, 106, 128; *see also* McNamara, Robert
defensive alliances, military aid to 45–46
de Gaulle, Charles 15, 101, 119
democracy, representative 77, 82
Democracy in America 3; *see also* De Tocqueville, Alexis
Democratic Party 18, 103, 128
Democrats 32, 34, 36, 37, 41, 50, 53, 59, 61–62, 75, 104, 108, 124; complaints by 33, 39; congressional elections 76; criticism by 38, 60, 103; partisan attack 62–63
Departments of Defense 89, 126
Destroyers Deal 11; *see also* Great Britain
De Tocqueville, Alexis 3

Detroit Free Press 130
Diem, Ngo Dinh 38, 71, *72*, 73, 76–78, 80, 81, 82, 83, 88, 91, 96, 120, 121; anti–Buddhist policies 93; assassination of 96, 118; coup against 98, 126; government of, American support for 73–74, 75, 82, 95, 96; stabilizing conditions in Vietnam 75, 91
Dien Bien Phu: air raid on 43; battle of 31–32, 35, 36, 39, 41–42, 58, 66, 101; fall of 60
diplomatic relations 20, 64, 98, 132
diplomats 11, 97
Dirksen, Sen. Everett 27, 37, 104, 115, 120, 122, 124, 128, 129
disputes: arbitration of 9; international 10
division of power 11; *see also* Senate
Dodd, Sen. Thomas 86, 90, 103, 129
domino theory 19, 20, 22, 23, 28, 37, 39, 40, 78, 118, 132; *see also* Truman, Harry S
Douglas, Paul 25
Douglas, William 72; *see also* Supreme Court Justice
Dulles, John Foster 24–25, 28, 31, 34, 35, 36, 37, 39, *40*, 41, 44, 46–49, 50–51, 53, 55, 56, 58–59, 61–63, 76, 137n11
Dutton, Frederick 97

economic assistance: to the French 20–21; Indochina 22; North Vietnam 81; Saigon 74; South Vietnam 2, 80, 107; Southeast Asia 91; Vietnam 24, 80–81, 105, 107
economy, the emergence of a national 9
Eden, British Foreign Secretary Anthony 49, 52, 53, 68; *see also* British foreign secretary
Eisenhower, Pres. Dwight 1, 2, 14, 18, 24, 28, 29–30, 31–35, 37, 39, *40*, 41, 42–44, 45–47, 50–51, 53, 56, 58, 63, 68, *72*, 73–74, 76, 80, 82, 83, 85, 94, 98, 118, 131, 136n18; administration 24–25, 29, 31–32, 45–46, 50, 58, 69–70, 71–76, 130
elected representatives 24, 103
elections: congressional 76; 1956 76–77; presidential 117, 118
elite forces 32
Ellender, Senator 120
England 15, 48, 53, 58

147

Index

En-lai, Chou 65, 69; *see also* Chinese foreign minister
Ervin, Sen. Sam 108
Europe: battleground of the Cold War 71; international army in 18, 19, 23; Locarno Pact 53; western coalition in 43, 66–67
European Defense Community 38, 58, 67, 68; French National Assembly's approval for the 59
European nations, military aid to 19, 63
executive agreements 10–11; *see also* Supreme Court
executive initiatives 3; abuses of 19
executive officer 10
executive power, use of 4, 10, 29, 106
export trade 5

fait accompli, danger of 13, 132; *see also* Fulbright, J. William; Johnson, Lyndon
Far Eastern Affairs, Assistant Secretary of State for 60; *see also* Robertson, Walter
Far Eastern Munich 58, 60
Federal Bureau of Investigation 11
federal system 9
Ferguson, Homer 40, 59, 66
Flanders, Ralph 16, 25, *27*, 39
Fleming, Denna 3
foreign aid 38, 48, 61, 63, 69, 73, 80; scandals in Vietnam 81, 82
foreign affairs: branches of government in 2, 3, 4, 131; co-equality with the president in 13, 113; executive's responsibilities 89; president's conduct 9, 10, 100–101; senate's authority 100, 113;
foreign control, independence from 28
foreign ministers: appointing 4; conference 58, 59
foreign policy: American 62, 85, 132; bipartisan 18; Democratic attack on the 50; execution of 29; executive initiatives 6–7, 17, 35, 100; hawk on 25, *28*; presidential control of 76, 89; role of the Senate 106, 131–132; shaping 1
Foreign Relations Committee 23, 24, 35, 54, 60, 82, 97, 115, 132, 137*n*20, 138*n*15
Formosa 19, 52, 76; crisis of 1955 112; *see also* Taiwan
founding fathers 13
France 14–15, 20, 22, 23, 31, 41, 45, 47–48, 53, 58, 62, 63, 75, 102, 104, 119;
and the Associated States 22, 26–27, 35, 62, 64; fighting in Indochina 38–39, 70; government 26; military aid to 17, 49, 69; military expenditures 70; Navarre Plan 31, 58; peace movement in 58; public opinion in 59, 61; withdrew forces from Vietnam 75; *see also* SEATO alliance
Franklin, Benjamin 1
free world 35, 37, 39, 46; allies 48; in Asia 94; nations 51, 52; U.S. leadership 63
French Communist Party 16
French government 16, 25, 48, 58; aid appropriation 27
French missionaries 14
French National Assembly 59
French Union troops 39, 73
French war: the battle of Cao Bay 17
Fulbright, Sen. J. William 12–13, 83, 85–86, 104–105, 108–109, 111–*112*, 113, 124, 127, 129

Geneva Accords 54, 88; terms 76
Geneva Conference 31, 39, 44, 47, 48–49, 50, 57, 58–70, 71, 87, 101, 137*n*7
George, Walter 32
Germany 53; Nazi 58
Gillette, Guy 25, 62
Goldman, Eric (historian) 100–101
Goldwater, Sen. Barry 26, 27, *102*, 104, 107, 111, 117, 128
GOP disasters 18
Gore, Sen. Albert 82
Goulden, Joseph (historian) 115
government: control 8; Mandarin philosophy 77; pro–American 16
Graebner, Norman 18
Grant, Ulysses 8
Great Britain 5, 9, 45, 54, 56, 61, 106; French and Indian war with 17; *see also* SEATO alliance
Great Lakes, naval limitations on the 6
Greece 2, 87, 106
Greek civil war 20
Greene, Theodore 62
Gruening, Sen. Ernest 100, *101*, 103, 105, 108, 111, 113, 116, 123, 127, 129
Guam 120
guerrilla war 17, 19, 42, 87, 101, 127

Hamilton, Alexander 4, 5
Hanoi 92, 93, 123, 128

148

Index

Hawaii, annexing of 9
Helvidius letters 5; *see also* Madison, James
Hennings, Sen. Thomas 76
Herring, George (historian) 77, 94
Hickenlooper, Sen. Burke 97
Hilsman, Roger 88, 90, 93, 98
Hinkle, Warren 73
Hitler, Adolf 126
Hoar, George 8
Hoover, Herbert 18–19, 43
House Armed Services Committee 101
Humphrey, Sen. Hubert 39, *64*, 75, 78, 89–90, 108
hydrogen bomb, impact of 68

India 19, 20, 39, 49, 51, 52, 68, 78, 82; *see also* Nehru, Prime Minister Jawaharlal
Indian War 17
Indians, treaty with the southern 4
Indochina 14–16, 20, 24, 58, 138*n*11; city of Haiphong 17, 128; collapse of French position in 66; Communist rebels 43, 49, 56, 60; crisis of 1954 31–32; defense 69; halting Japanese expansion 28; Japanese seizure 14–15; political guide 82; transport French Union troops to 39; unification 79; U.S. position 19, 23, 25–26, 28, 37–38, 43, 49, 55, 59, 62–63, 68, 69
Indochina War 17, 31–34, 45
Indochinese Communist Party 16, 26
Indochinese peace settlement 67
Indonesia 19, 52, 78
international justice 22
international politics 9, 12
intervention: American 35, 37–40, 42, 45, 47, 51, 61, 68, 108; armed 41; non-intervention 42; unilateral 31, 49, 106; western 60
Italy 53

Jackson, Sen. Henry 37, 91, 92
Japan 17, 19, 78
Javits, Sen. Jacob 80, 102, 108, *127*, 128–129, 132–133, 140*n*2
Jay, John 11
Jay Treaty 5
Jefferson, Thomas 5, 12
Jenner, William 49–50
Johnson, Edwin 40, 69
Johnson, Pres. Lyndon 1, 2, 12, 46, 50, 62, 83, 85, 89, 91, 96, 100–101, 105, 106, 117–118, *119*, 120–121, 124–*125*, 126, 127, 129, 130; administration 16, 101–103, 105, 108, 109, 111, 116, 117, 118, 121–124, 127, 128; John Hopkins University speech 123–24, 131; signs Tonkin Gulf Resolution *115*
Joint Chiefs of Staff 22, 33, 36; protests 69, 128
joint resolution 36; *see also* Congress

Kahin, George, Historian 75, 97
Kai-shek, Chiang 15–16
Keating, Sen. Kenneth 83, 102–103
Kefauver, Estes 38, 50, 63
Kelly, Edna 73
Kennedy, John F. 1, 2, 25–26, 36, 69, 71–73, 78–79, 83; as president 84–99, *87*, 106, 118, 130–131
Kennedy, Sen. Joseph P. 25–26, 36, 42, 69, 71, 129
Khan, Gen. Nguyen 105, 121
Khrushchev, Nikita 85
Knowland, Sen. William 25, *28*, 29, 32, 37, 41, 46, 48–49, 50, 52, 59–60, 62, 64, 65, 69
Korea 2, 18–19, 23, 25, 35, 38, 46, 49, 59, 60, 77, 81, 120; U.S. commander in 42
Korean War 12, 16, 18, 20, 30, 35, 118; American entry into the 17, 38
Kuchel, Sen. Thomas 95
Ky, Marshall Nguyan Cao 126

Landon, Alfred 18
Laos 22, 25, 26, 41, 49, 50, 54, 62, 64, 68, 87, 102, 108, 118, 122; Ho Chi Minh trail 120; Loatian crisis 84–85
Latin America 6, 63, 90
Lausche, Sen. Frank 120
law of nations 4
law of the land *see* executive agreements; Supreme Court
Lebanon, crisis of 112
legislative duties 8
legislative leaders 41
legislative supremacy, theory of 3; *see also* Locke, John
legislatures, colonial 3
Lend Lease Act 11; *see also* Congress
Lerche, Charles 52, 137*n*16
Lerner, Max 73
Lewis, political analyst 97

149

Index

liberty 12, 95
Life magazine 16, 72
Lincoln, Pres. Abraham 7, 8, 10
Locarno, Treaty of 52; Locarno Pact 53
Locke, John 3
Lodge, Henry Cabot 96
London 5, 39, 48
Long, Sen. Russell 124
Lovett, Robert 24

MacArthur, Gen. Douglas 42, 98
Maclay, Senator 4
Maddox, destroyer 109
Madison, James 4, 5, 6, 12
Malaya 19, 45, 51
Manchuria 41
Mansfield, Sen. Mike 1, 24, 27, 28, 32, 40, 52, 61, 65–66, 72, 73, 77, 78, 79–80, 81–82, 89, 90, 91, 96, 98, 101, 102, 109, ***119***, 120, 121, 124, 129, 138*n*14, 138*n*15
Marshall Plan 17, 54
mass media 11
McCarren, Sen. Pat 53, 65
McCarthy, Sen. Joseph 73
McGee, Sen. Gale 82, 123, 127
McGovern, Sen. George 95, 119, 121, 122
McKinley, William 9
McNamara, Defense Sec. Robert ***87***, 90, 96, 101, 105–107, 120, 124, ***125***, 128
Mendes-France, Pierre 64, 65, 67
Mexico 7–8
Middle East 2
military: aid/assistance 73–74, 80–81, 90–91, 107; alliance 49, 69; crisis 10, 24; operations 16, 22
Minh, Gen. Duong Van 100, 105, 121
Minh, Ho Chi 14, 16–17, 20, 26, 28, 61, 68, 75, 78, 79, 120; *see also* Laos
Minister of the Interior 71; *see also* Diem, Ngo Dinh
Molotov, Vyachev 69; *see also* Russian foreign minister
monks, Buddhist 95, 96
Monroe, Pres. James 6
Monroe Doctrine 6, 10, 52, 55, 62
Morganthau, Hans 56–57
Morse, Sen. Wayne 22, 51, 91, 95, 100, 103, 105–107, 108, 111, ***112***, 113, 115, 116, 123, 129
Moscow 26

Munich 41, 101
Mutual Security Act 26

nation, politics of the 9; interests of the 34
national emergency 8
national policies 9, 33–35, 76
national unity 76
nationalist 71, 74, 77, 98
naval force, reduction in 66
Navarre, Henri 31–32, 58; *see also* Vietnam, Navarre military strategy for
Nehru, Prime Minister Jawaharlal 49, 52; *see also* India
Nehru Doctrine 82; *see also* Indochina
Nelson, Sen. Gaylord 113–***114***
Neuberger, Richard 73
Neutrality Act 5, 10
New Look defense policy 33, 43, 57, 66, 85; *see also* Eisenhower, Pres. Dwight
New York Herald Tribune 72, 80
The New York Times 21, 22, 24, 42, 43, 50, 51, 59, 61, 63, 69, 72, 76–77, 80, 81–82, 87, 96, 98, 109, 115, 122
New Zealand 45, 46, 52; *see also* SEATO alliance
Nhu, Madame 94
Nhu, Ngo Dinh 77, 93, 94; assassination of 96
Nixon, Richard, Vice President 28, 39, 41, 49, 136*n*12
North Africa 19
North American Review 8; *see also* Wilson, Woodrow
North Atlantic Pact 17, 19
North Atlantic Treaty Organization (NATO) 23, 38, 48, 53, 54, 55, 59, 67; *see also* European Defense Community
North Vietnam 70, 76, 103, 105, 107, 118, 123; air strikes on 121, 123; American bombing attack on 109, 121; land reform program in 79
North Vietnamese government 82–83
nuclear: test ban 88; weapons 36

O'Donnell, Kenneth 98
Olney-Pauncefote Treaty 9

Pacific NATO 49
Pacific Treaty Organization 49–50
Pakistan 52; *see also* SEATO alliance
Panama Canal 9
Panama Congress 6

150

Index

Paris 39, 48
Paris Peace Conference 16
Parliament 50
partisanship 18, 37, 50, 60, 62, 88–89, 114, 128
peace, achievement of 5, 12, 39, 47, 48, 53–55, 58, 61, 63–64, 66–67, 69, 79, 81, 108, 111, 118, 124
Pearl Harbor 12, 15, 122
Peking 59, 60, 66, 127
Pell, Sen. Claiborne 91, 108, 138n15
Pentagon 111
the *Pentagon Papers* 77, 84, 96, 97, 98, 105, 111
Pepper, Claude 22
persecution, religious 95; *see also* Buddhists
Philippine Treaty 45
Philippines 1, 19, 47, 49, 54, 78, 120; *see also* SEATO alliance
Pierce, Pres. Franklin 7
Poland 68
policymakers, State Department 18, 93, 97
political struggles, Third World 98
Polk, Pres. James 7
Potomac Charter 53
Potter, Ralph 25, 26
power: balance of 19; debate over executive's 34–35; equitable distribution 4; war-making 12, 55–56, 111
powers: constitutional 10, 55, 76, 105; president's 10, 55
presidency: historical powers 76; "stewardship" 10
presidential authority, defense of the 6
presidents: administrations 5, 130; modern 11
Prime Minister 47; *see also* Churchill, Winston; Dai, Bao 73
Proxmire, Sen. William 123
public opinion 11, 35; for nonintervention 41

Quebec 17

Radford, William 33, 34, 36
reforms: land 79; social and political 71, 74, 94
relations, foreign 10
Republican National Committee 88
Republican Party 18, 20, 62, 107; advanced internationalists 59–60

Republicans 5, 17, 19, 20, 23, 29, 37–38, 40, 43, 48, 50–51, 53, 59, 61, 63, 88, 90, 102, 103, 118, 120, 122, 124, 128; task force 107–109
Reston, James 43, 51
revolutionary patriots 3
Ridgeway, Matthew 42, 136n19
Ridgway report 42–43, 85
Roberts, Chalmers 43
Robertson, Walter 60, 78
Roman Catholicism 14
Roosevelt, Theodore 9, 29, 43, 66, 135n16; world policeman theory 15
Roosevelt Corollary 10; *see also* Monroe Doctrine
Rostow, Walt 87
Rush-Bagot agreement 6
Rusk, Sec. of State Dean 108, 114, 116, 124, **125**, 139n1
Russell, Sen. Richard 32, 109, 112, 125–26, 129, 131
Russia 16, 20, 43, 46, 47, 59, 60, 68, 69, 79, 88, 97
Russian foreign minister 69; *see also* Molotov, Vyachev

Saigon 24, 73, 74, 79, 81, 83, 86, 93–94, 95, 96, 106, 117, 118, 128, 129
The St. Louis *Post-Dispatch* 95
Saltonstall, Sen. Leverett 25, 107
Santa Domingo (Haiti) 8
scandals, foreign aid 81–83
Scheer, Robert 73
Schlesinger, Arthur, Jr. (historian) 73, 87–88, 90, 97
Scott, Sen. Hugh 123
Secretary of State 35, 36, 41, 46, 49–50, 61–63, 66, 78, 93, 97, 116, 125
Secretary of War 4
Senate: concurrence 9; congressional review of the war in South Vietnam 102–103; consent of the 4, 42, 54–55, 66, 95, 113; constitutional authority in foreign affairs 100; demands for clarification of the government's policy 39, 59, 61, 88, 91; diversity 11, 120, 124; domestic political backlash 69; foreign policy initiative 130; hostile to Diem regime 94–95; lack of consensus 121; opposition from 31, 32–33, 35, 37–38, 40, 43, 49, 58, 64, 66, 88, 100, 105–107, 129; opposition to the Tonkin Gulf Resolution 111, 117, 122; protests

151

Index

by 69, 95, 132; revolt by 14, 17; role in the creation of SEATO 45, 49, 50, 52, 56; tour of Vietnam 91; unification in Vietnam 81, 132; winning approval of 30, 37; *see also* Foreign Relations Committee
Senate Armed Services Committee 25; *see also* Saltonstall, Leverett
Senate Foreign Relations Committee 10, 23, 24, 33, 35, 54, 60, 82, 97, 115, 132, 137*n*20, 138*n*15
Senate Judiciary Committee 29
Senate Majority Leader 29, 83; *see also* Johnson, Lyndon; Knowland, William
Senate Republican Policy Committee; *see also* Ferguson, Homer
ships, arm merchant 10
Singapore 19
64th Federalist (1788) 11
slavery 8, 77
Smathers, Sen. George 63, 111
Smith, Sen. Alexander 50, 56, 59, 60, 63, 91
Smith, Sen. Benjamin 138*n*15
Smith, Walter Bedell 32, 34, 40, 66
Sorenson, Ted 97, 98
South Korea 19, 46, 47, 52; Communist attack 22
South Vietnam 2, 45, 54, 56, 64, 74, 79, 105, 121, 123; American commitment 86, 93, 100, 122–23; bring democracy to 82; Buddhist crisis 93; halt spread of Communism 71, 83, 90–91, 125; neutralization policy 105, 118; non–Communist forces 67–68, 126 preserve freedom 104; U.S. aid 70, 80–82, 85, 87, 100, 105, 125, 139*n*15; U.S. involvement 87–89, 102, 107, 117, 126–27; U.S. Marines in 123, 126; withdrawal from 94–95, 103, 127
South Vietnamese Army 126–127
Southeast Asia 17, 20–22, 24, 27, 33, 35, 37–39, 42, 46, 56, 77–78, 114–115; against Communist encroachment in 80, 108; collective security system for 41, 46, 50–52, 78, 118; defense pact 48, 53, 67, 70; protect American interests in 91, 109, 117, 120; regional defense organization 47, 51–52, 54, 61; Tonkin Gulf crisis 100, 111; U.S. aid 91; U.S. military involvement 84, 90, 98–99, 103, 107, 111, 113, 117, 123
Southeast Asia Treaty Organization (SEATO) 44, 45–57, 86–87, 122; Article IV 55; *see also* Pacific Treaty Organization
Soviet Union 15, 21, 40, 60, 64, 77, 85
Spain 19
Spanish-American War 1, 9
Sparkman, Sen. John 83, 106
Spellman, Francis Cardinal 71
State Department 21, 95, 97, 126
statesmanship 9, 80
statutes 10
Stennis, Sen. John 32, **33**, 34, 36, 37, 39, 109
Stevenson, Adlai 34
Stimson, Sec. of State Henry L. 41
Suez Canal 19
Sumner, Charles 8
Supreme Court 11; Belmont decision 11; Curtiss-Wright decision (1936) 11
Supreme Court Justice 72; *see also* Douglas, William
Symington, Sen. Stuart 69, 91, 92

Taft, Robert 19–20, **23**
Taiwan 47, 76; *see also* Formosa
Taylor, Gen. Maxwell 81, **87**, 88, 98, 118, 128
Texas 7; *see also* Tyler, John
Thailand 19, 47, 49, 54, 78; *see also* SEATO alliance
Thomas, Norman 73
Thuc, Ngo Dinh 77
Thurmond, Sen. Strom 121
Time magazine 72
"Titoism" 26
To Move a Nation 98; *see also* Hilsman, Roger
Tokyo 71
Tonkin Gulf 101, 109, 117
Tonkin Gulf Resolution 100, 111, **112**, 116, 122, 125–26, 127; amendment to 113–115
Tower, Senator 129
trade embargo 15
treaties 4, 5, 23, 28, 45, 52, 55, 106
Tripoli 6
troop commitments 19, 22–25, 29, 30, 32–33, 37, 42, 45, 49, 52, 70, 85, 87–88, 98, 108–109, 117, 120, 123, 126, 129
Truman, Pres. Harry 12, 16–20, **21**, 22, 25, 29, 36, 87, 94, 106, 118, 131
Truman Doctrine 17, 21, 87

152

Index

trusteeships, international 15
Tse-tung, Mao 65
Turkey 2, 106
Twining, Nathan 36
Tydings, Joseph 61
Tyler, John 6–7

Undersecretary of State 90; *see also* Hilsman, Roger
unified action 35–36, 39, 41, 46, 61–62; in Southeast Asia 48, 63; in Vietnam 50, 81
United Nations 17, 22, 24, 36, 38, 43, 45, 46, 60, 64–66, 128
United States: dominant Western power 70; integrity of 111; member of SEATO 54; president of 13, 26, 29, 35, 43, 84; prestige of 29, 65, 79, 126; Republican support 38; security of 43, 103
U.S. Army 87
United States Constitution 111
United States Founding Fathers 112
U.S.-French partnership 69
United States government 3, 21, 45, 56–57, 59, 62–63, 67, 68, 72, 96; assists government of Vietnam 73–74; mutual security program 83; policy in Vietnam 82, 125
The United States in Vietnam 97
U.S. International Cooperation Administration 82
U.S. Marines 123, 126
U.S. military protection 2, 20–22, 69–70
U.S. presidents 1, 2, 84; prerogatives and responsibilities 89, 95, 106, 108
U.S. Senate: on foreign policy 106–107, 132–133; role 1–2
unity, appeals for 19, 60

Vandenberg, Arthur 18
Vandenberg Resolution 45
Van Fleet, Gen. James A. 87
Van Thieu, Gen. Nguyan 126
Versailles, rejection of the Treaty of 10
victory, price of 103
Vietnam 15, 17, 22, 23, 26, 31, 39, 42, 49, 62, 64, 68, 73, 77–78, 80–81, 96, 128; agriculture in 79, 81; American friends of 73; American stake in 78–79; American war in 91–92; Communist threat 85, 123; diplomatic solution 46; dominant Western power 70; government 73, 78; independence 16, 72, 74, 81, 86; Japanese incursions into 16; Navarre military strategy 58; non–Communism 73, 78; power struggle 75; unified nation 68; unilateral American intervention in 49, 106; U.S. role in 93–94, 116, 117, 122–23, 125, 131; *see also* Southeast Asia Treaty Organization
Vietnam War 1, 12, 31–32
Vietnamese Embassy 24
Vietnamese Emperor 20, 73; *see also* Dai, Bao
violent threat 4
V-J Day 80
votes, Democratic 29

war: act of 36; declaration of 56, 107, 111, 113; disadvantage to America 43
war and peace, determination of 3, 5, 12, 68, 111
war vessels, foreign 5, 111
Washington, Pres. George 4–5, 51
The Washington Post 80
Washington Star 18
Watkins, Ralph 35–36
weapons: atomic 107; nuclear 120
Welles, Sumner 15
Western Europe 2
Western European alliance 15, 59
Westmoreland, Gen. William 126
White, William S. 42
White House 8, 41, 46, 95, 97, 122, 128
Wicker, Tom 109, 122
Wiley, Alexander 35, 63, 69
Wilson, Defense Secretary Charles 34, 41
Wilson, Pres. Woodrow 8, 9, 10
world affairs, leadership in 29
World Court 10
world order, preserve 15
World War I 10, 53
World War II 1, 10, 14, 17, 20, 53, 63, 94; post–World War II era 2, 12–13, 14–30, 87, 130, 132

Yalta Conference 15
Young, Sen. Allen 111

www.ingramcontent.com/pod-product-compliance
Ingram Content Group UK Ltd.
Pitfield, Milton Keynes, MK11 3LW, UK
UKHW042017140426
5217IPUK00015B/1217